Eating Your Way Across

Eating Your Way Across

KENTUCKY

101 MUST PLACES to EAT

Gary P. West

FOREWORD BY **Byron Crawford**

ACCLAIM PRESS
Morley, Missouri

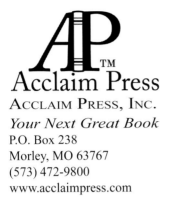

Acclaim Press

ACCLAIM PRESS, INC.
Your Next Great Book
P.O. Box 238
Morley, MO 63767
(573) 472-9800
www.acclaimpress.com

Book Design by:

Designer: Mary Ellen Sikes
Cover Design: Emily K. Sikes

Publishing Rights: Acclaim Press

Library of Congress Catalog No.: 2006935999
ISBN: 0-9790025-1-6
Printed in the United States of America
Fifth printing: October 2007
10 9 8 7 6 5

Additional copies may be purchased from
Acclaim Press.

This publication was produced using available information. The Publisher regrets it cannot assume
responsibility for errors or omissions.

Contents

Dedication

This book is dedicated to all of the hard working people in the restaurant industry, not just the owners and managers, but the chefs, cooks and servers. Some of these incredible people have worked in this business for decades, always giving of their time, energy and wonderful personality. Most make you feel like they are truly glad you are there. I have never been called "Sugar", "Hon" or "Baby" as much as when I researched this book.

To these people, this book is dedicated.

Foreword

Just when you thought Gary West could never match his last book, *King Kelly Coleman*, a fascinating biography of Kentucky's greatest basketball legend, he has come up with a subject even more dear to the hearts of Kentuckians than basketball—good food!

The book's appetizing title, *Eating Your Way Across Kentucky*, invites the question: "Why didn't I think of that?"

West--who is as gifted with a pen as with a knife, fork and spoon--has artfully sampled the most delicious fare of many of Kentucky's historic inns, family restaurants, tea rooms, diners and country stores from the Big Sandy to the Mississippi.

Those of us who criss-cross Kentucky for a living have always known that many of the best eateries are off the beaten path, where they seldom gain much notice beyond a local clientele.

West takes particular care to include these great places in his tasteful mix of upscale and down-home dining establishments. Drawing on his boyhood memories of internationally famous, Bowling Green food critic Duncan Hines, West personally visited all of the 101 restaurants featured in this book before recommending them to others.

If Duncan Hines were with us today, he'd likely have this book on his reading table.

You will find it to be much more than a directory of good places to eat. It is also a keepsake history of people, places and Kentucky menus in these times that should be passed along to your children and grandchildren.

The restaurant names alone are worth the reading—the "Atomic Café" in Lexington, "Beehive" in Augusta, "Chat-n-Nibble" in Eminence, "Greyhound Tavern" in Fort Mitchell, "Hot Diggity-Dog" in Cadiz, "Miss Ida's Tea Room" in Inez, "The Purple Onion" in Central City.

From comfort foods to fancy dining; from "Weaver's Hot Dogs" in London, to "The Glitz" in Nonesuch, and from the "Old Stone Inn" in

Simpsonville, to "Missy's Out of the Way Café" in Raywick, West has compiled an entertaining field guide to fantastic foods across the Commonwealth.

All you need do is keep your bookmark out of the butter, and come hungry!

–Byron Crawford
Kentucky Collumnist
The Courier-Journal

Preface

If you are expecting a traveling gourmet guide, this is not it. If you are expecting a list of places to get good food at reasonable prices, this is your book!

The only real way to experience the cuisine that is unique to Kentucky is to do it bite by bite.

This is a book that can direct you to good eating if you choose to stay on the interstate or good eating if you take to the back roads.

The book is not designed for gourmet dining or candlelight dinners, although you very well may find a little of both at some of our locations.

It's all about simple food!

It's important to know that none of the eateries in this book paid for their inclusion. The only way a restaurant made our "101 list" was to be recommended by someone who lives in the area, often people in the tourism and hospitality business. The restaurant was then qualified personally by the author or trusted associates.

The end result is a handy guide to "101 Must Places to Eat."

My wife, Deborah, and I criss-crossed the state to the tune of approximately 5,200 miles. For both of us it was an incredible experience, winding around narrow back roads, often looking for that certain landmark the fellow at the filling station had told us where to turn.

Many weekends over a two year period were taken up by our travels. Sometimes we would head out on a Thursday morning and return home on a Sunday evening, visiting as many as four restaurants in a single day. What a life!

The scenery in Kentucky is awesome. From the flatlands, to the rolling hills to the breathtaking mountains, we sometime missed turns and road signs because of looking at the beauty surrounding us. But that was okay. I became pretty good at backing up and turning around.

I can't remember how many times we crossed the Kentucky River. Surely there's more than one, there just has to be.

The glistening lakes could put you in a trance with the sun sparkling on the dancing waves, but so could a neat little farm pond framed by a little white house, and old silo and a nearby country church.

Beauty is, indeed in the eye of the beholder.

Several years ago, while traveling in a nearby state, I ran across the sort of beauty I'm talking about.

The place looked interesting enough. An old house converted into a restaurant. Not a spot I would have picked on my own but the locals said it was good. Why not?

The plastic covered menus with the metal corner protectors were evidence they wanted these no frills menus to last for a while. It was the usual fare, chicken, chops, steaks, and fish. The waiter suggested the steaks. Why not?

After chomping through a so-so lettuce salad, the steak and a hearty order of golden brown steak fries arrived. The waiter assured us that there would be no need for steak sauce. But you should have seen the look on his face when we asked for catsup for those fries. He rolled his eyes, clinched his teeth and quickly glanced over his shoulders in both directions as if to make sure no one was listening.

"The cook's not gonna like it if you put catsup on 'em" he whispered, nodding to my plate.

I quickly replied that I was the one paying for it and I didn't care what the cook thought. Bring me some catsup.

Seconds later, as if a Hollywood central casting department were involved, a stocky fellow wearing white pants, a sleeveless undershirt covered by a semi-white apron, with an assortment of stains, some of which sure did look alot like blood, arrived at my table. In one hand was a meat cleaver. The hand could have easily held a bottle of catsup. But it didn't. In a not so friendly voice he asked, "Is there a problem?"

Suddenly I realized I didn't need catsup after all.

Would I go back there? You're darn right I would. The steak was good and those fries were some of the best I've ever eaten. But more important, for years it has provided me with a story to tell.

Driving Blindly

Igrew up hearing about Duncan Hines. My dad was a traveling sales-man in the late 40s, and my mom and I would accompany him during the summer months until we returned to Kentucky in time for me to start school. More often than not when traveling we all looked for the "Recommended by Duncan Hines" signs in order to decide where we ate and spent the night. There were only a handful of chain motels and res-taurants at this time, so one of the Duncan Hines signs was most coveted. It often determined the success or failure of a diner or lodge.

This particular summer took us through the Carolinas and Virginia on two lane roads, as interstates were still on the drawing boards.

"Don't pass him, you'll get us all killed," my ever-cautious mother screamed to my dare devil-driving dad.

Sitting in the back seat of the two-door, 1948 Chevy, paying no par-ticular interest to anything, the word "killed" got my attention. Being six-years-old and with no seat belt to unsnap or restraint straps to unhook, I sprang to the center opening of the two front seats, gripping them hard to pull myself up as close as possible.

Directly in front of our car, plainly visible through our front wind-shield, was the rear end of a black-paneled truck.

At this period of my life I was not a very good reader. But, I didn't have to be.

My mother read the big red letters for all of us.

"Do Not Pass, Blind Man Driving."

I still recall the excitement as I wondered how he did it. I even re-member shutting my eyes, only to quickly open them to see if we were still on the narrow road.

To pass or not to pass? For several miles it was a point of contention between my mom and dad. I never said a word, still wondering how the blind man did it.

Finally my dad, after what seemed like miles and miles, decided he had followed the slow moving truck long enough. With a straight stretch of clear sailing and no oncoming cars in sight, he stomped the gas pedal and announced he was passing. With my mother shouting, "Don't pass him, he's blind," my dad did it anyway.

As we pulled alongside the slow-moving truck, I'll never forget the neatly lettered sign on the side, "AAA Venetian Blind Sales."

My dad laughed and laughed, as if he knew it all along. My mom never said a word, as if someone had played a dirty trick on her.

The sign said "Blind Man Driving," and it was a blind man, but this one could see.

Something like this could only happen on the back roads, on a two lane road. It's stories like this that add to a lifetime of wonderful memories.

Introduction

There are literally thousands of eating-places in Kentucky. Some are outstanding, some good, some fair and some not so good. One would think it would be easy to identify "101 must places to eat" in the state. Normally it would be, but what I've done in these pages is to select eateries that in all probability you may not visit unless they are listed here. Oh sure, the locals eat there, but some of the restaurants are not well known to outsiders - - until now.

The criteria for making the 101 are that it cannot be a chain restaurant, and must have been in operation for at least five years. There are a few exceptions to the latter.

There are many fine restaurants, chains and independents, and their omission from this book is certainly not a reflection of their quality. It's just that this book, for the most part, gives you a guide to some of the other places.

The famous hospitality guru Duncan Hines, a Kentuckian from Bowling Green, first printed his dining recommendations in an easy to follow guidebook back in the late 1930's and continued it well into the 1950's. I have tried to duplicate what Mr. Hines did.

As people's travel habits changed with the building of interstates and increased popularity of air travel, the guidebooks lost their zest. But now there is a large segment of the population who is not quite as in a hurry as they once were. That's why it's time. It's time to get you off of the interstate and onto the wonderful back roads of Kentucky where there are mighty fine people to meet and mighty fine food to eat.

The state has been broken down into five regions that will make it easier for you to reference your travels. Along with each eatery will be some "touristy" type things to see and do in the area. It is suggested that if you are traveling a great distance to eat in one of the listed restaurants that you may want to call ahead to verify hours of operation. Remember time zone changes.

It is suggested that you always check to make sure these restaurants are open, particularly if you are making the trip solely for the dining experience. Because some of these restaurants are indeed "back roads" establishments, they sometime change their hours of operation. Some even shut down for seasonal breaks. In some cases this is noted.

The 101 restaurants in these pages are as diverse as the state itself.

Visitors unfamiliar with Kentucky laws should be aware that many counties throughout the state cannot legally sell alcohol.

At press time menu items were confirmed. These, too, change! Any directions given in this book are only for reference. You might want to stop and ask the locals for more specifics. This can be part of the fun and hopefully add to the experience.

Eating Your Way Across Kentucky

BOB'S DRIVE-IN   PADUCAH, KY
BRIARPATCH RESTAURANT   OWENSBORO, KY
CHARLIE'S STEAKHOUSE   OAK GROVE, KY
THE CUMBERLAND HOUSE   KUTTAWA, KY
DIFABIO'S   MADISONVILLE, KY
FERRELL'S HAMBURGERS   HOPKINSVILLE, KY
HIH BURGER   MURRAY, KY
HILL'S BAR-B-QUE   MAYFIELD, KY
HORSESHOE STEAKHOUSE   HOPKINSVILLE, KY
HOT DIGGITY DOG   CADIZ, KY
IVY'S FINE DINING   HARTFORD, KY
KIRCHHOFF'S BAKERY & DELI PADUCAH, KY
PATTI'S 1800 SETTLEMENT   GRAND RIVERS, KY
THE FEED MILL RESTAURANT   MORGANFIELD, KY
THE PELICAN RESTAURANT   LAKE CITY, KY
THE PURPLE ONION   CENTRAL CITY, KY
WOLF'S RESTAURANT & TAVERN HENDERSON, KY

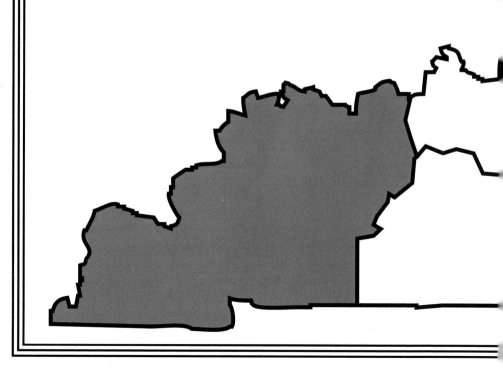

WESTERN REGION

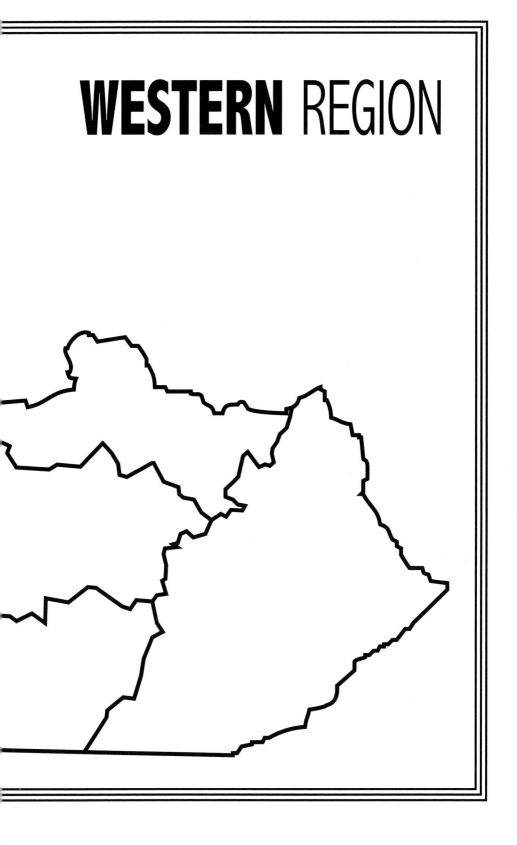

Bob's Drive-In
PADUCAH, KENTUCKY

A visit to Bob's Drive-In is like stepping back in time. And in this case it is good!

What started out in 1949 as a Dairy Queen eventually became a tradition in this Ohio River city when the original owner, Bob Holman, decided to drop the franchise and go on his own.

Neil Ward has owned Bob's for well over a quarter of a century but little has changed from the very beginning.

Thirty speakers recently updated from the original ones installed in 1957 are there for customers to call in their orders. And some even say Bob's still uses the same delivery trays that hang on car windows when they first opened.

The best thing of all, however, is that the food is still good, especially the two signature items.

The fiesta burger and foot long chili dog have been applauded for years. The fiesta burger is not for the faint of heart. It's a classic hamburger patty, topped with delicious home-made chili from a secret recipe. Nacho cheese sauce and onions are piled on top and sandwiched between the traditional Paducah toasted buns. All of a sudden you have a fiesta burger.

Bob's has an assortment of menu items as you would expect at a classic drive-in eatery.

Onion rings, tator tots, coleslaw, dog-on-a-stick, grilled chicken sandwiches,

18

and a selection of kids' meals all add to the eating experience at Bob's.

What would a drive-in restaurant be without the best milk shakes in town? Why not a pineapple shake, or a raspberry, or even a peanut butter! On top of this they have an assortment of shakes made from candies such as Heath Bars and M & M's. Straws are useless with them so that's why they'll give you a spoon.

DINERS INFORMATION

Address:
2429 Bridge Street
Hours:
Open, 10:00 a.m. – 10:00 p.m. daily, spring and summer
10:00 a.m. – 9:00 p.m. daily, fall and winter
Closed Sunday
Phone:
270/443-6493
Price Range: $
Area Attractions:
Quilters Museum, Flood Wall Murals, Gen. Lloyd Tilghman Civil War Museum

Briarpatch Restaurant

There aren't many pure "steak houses" left, but there's one in Owensboro, Kentucky. In a city that promotes itself as the barbeque capital of the world, the Briarpatch has managed to find a niche and stay there for some 35 years.

The Briarpatch is casual dining, yet it offers a classy touch, especially in the evening for those who want to recognize a special occasion. The open cooking, behind a clear glass partition, lets visitors see that this is a happening place. The cook's white jacket and white fluffy beret style headdress adds a nice flair to the scene.

Here, it all starts with an exceptional salad bar that includes Hoppin John soup that is almost as much of a tradition as the great steaks that are served. If there's a problem it's that the salad plates are too small.

Of course there's an assortment of steaks in various cuts and sizes. But also know the smoked pork loin is superb. It is marinated in a combination of pineapple, ginger, soy, worchester, brown sugar and garlic. Wow!

Two of the more popular seafood items are the Polynesian Tuna and Shrimp New Orleans.

An assortment of appetizers and side dishes as well as desserts are on the menu.

A lunch menu offers a wide choice of burgers, beef and, of course, hot browns.

The Briarpatch, a dining staple in Owensboro since 1971,

is not on the main drag of restaurants, but you will not be sorry you made the extra effort to locate it.

"We've kept our standards high, serving quality food at a fair price," offers owner Pat Buntin.

Address:
2760 Veach Road
Hours:
Open, Lunch, Sunday – Friday, 11:00 a.m. – 2:00 p.m.
Dinner, Sunday – 4:00 p.m. – 8:30 p.m.
Monday – Thursday, 5:00 p.m. – 9:30 p.m.
Friday & Saturday, 5:00 p.m. – 10:30 p.m.
Phone:
270/685-3329
Price Range: $$
Area Attractions:
Motor Sports/Festivals, Bluegrass Music Museum

Charlie's Steakhouse

OAK GROVE, KENTUCKY

Since April 8, 1952, Charlie's, just across the street from Ft. Campbell, has been serving the largest steaks you'll find anywhere. There's something about the feel of the glass block opening of the front door combined with an old-fashioned diner look that makes for an upscale atmosphere.

Like many good restaurants throughout Kentucky, the outside of the restaurant is nothing to get excited about, just a big steer on top of the building that says "Charlie's." But once inside it all changes. Cloth napkins, candles on the table and background music you are aware of, but still let you enjoy a conversation.

With that said prepare yourself for a dining experience. This legendary steak place serves up a 30-ounce porterhouse on a sizzling plate that literally hangs over the sides. Don't even think about one person eating the whole thing. And to go with it, the biggest, roundest baked potato you've ever seen in your life.

The salad they serve before the steak arrives should have been a clue. It, too, is huge. Blended in with the lettuce are beets, mushrooms, cabbage, carrots, bacon and almonds. You have your choice of homemade honey mustard and vinaigrette. But the best of all is the homemade blue cheese. Don't leave Charlie's without tasting it.

Charlie's serves other things in large portions- - like their lobster, shrimp and a 24-ounce "man-size" sirloin, and the vegetable soup is just like mom used to make, delicious.

A full service bar and extensive wine list is available.

DINERS INFORMATION

Address:
Hwy. 41 (near Ft. Campbell)
Hours:
Open, 4:00 p.m. – 10:00 p.m., Monday – Saturday
Closed Sunday
Phone:
270/439-4592
Price Range: $$
Area Attractions:
Ft. Campbell

23

The Cumberland House

"I can't believe buffet food can taste this good," one customer was overheard to say. "I'm coming back for the seafood tomorrow night," said another. That's how good this restaurant in the lake region of Western Kentucky really is, and it's only open three nights a week: Thursday, Friday and Saturday nights.

The restaurant has a nautical theme with a life-size mannequin of Captain Jim sitting in the lobby greeting customers. But the real Captain Jim is owner and operator Jim Emily, who has created a restaurant that has perhaps flown under the radar screen.

Captain Jim has a fun place to eat, especially during the warm weather months. With 110 seats inside and another 75 on a covered deck that features a full service bar, customers can enjoy entertainment on a stage nearby. Great atmosphere.

But the real reason you go to the Cumberland house is the food. Like the prime rib buffet on Friday nights. Or the unbelievable seafood buffet Saturday nights. Wow!

The meal starts at the salad bar that is a converted grocery store cooler with all good stuff set in it, including chilled bowls (not plates) and even chilled forks. It's a nice touch. You won't ever see bigger slices of mushrooms and cucumbers than here.

The buffet, not only has prime rib, but also beef brisket, and bar-b-que ribs. Sit-

ting nearby is a big bowl of real horseradish. The sidekicks include brown-sugar-laced bar-b-que beans, scalloped potatoes, fried cream corn, real homemade mashed potatoes and asparagus.

The seafood buffet has all of its fried items hand breaded in a special breading. There's oysters Rockefeller, seafood stuffed mushrooms, Cajun crawfish boil, shrimp scampi, shrimp fettuccini, baked grouper, fresh vegetables, smoked oysters, boiled shrimp, baked salmon, portabella mushrooms, clam chowder and Alaskan Snow Crab Legs.

Other menu items include rib eye steak, chicken breast, spaghetti and fried shrimp. An extensive wine list makes it complete.

DINERS INFORMATION

Directions:
Turn right at Kuttawa Exit on Hwy. 62 West and go four miles. Turn at The Cumberland House.
Open:
Thur. - Sat., 5:00 p.m. - 9:00 p.m., March 15 – Labor Day
Phone:
270/388-7722
Price Range:$$
Area Attractions:
Kentucky Lake

DiFabio's
MADISONVILLE, KENTUCKY

The green and red awning at 17 West Center Street screams at you that this is an Italian restaurant. But what you don't find out until you go inside is that it is an outstanding Italian restaurant.

DiFabio's is a family owned restaurant that has been around for a while. It offers a full service bar with enough room for four people to enjoy a beverage while waiting for a table, or you can sit there and enjoy good conversation with owners Peter and Laura DiFabio.

The atmosphere here is strictly Italian especially when Dean Martin croons out some of his old standards. How much better can it get?

Customers immediately notice the efficient wait staff and are impressed with their knowledge of the various wines and, of course, the menu. You don't always see this.

A good way to start is with the stuffed baked mushroom caps. Oh my! They're stuffed with breadcrumbs, parmesan cheese, spinach and mushrooms. Then there are the baked scallops, perhaps the best you've ever tasted. Other starters are baked escargot, toasted ravioli and spinach artichoke dip.

The entrees are really special at DiFabio's. Scallops, salmon, spaghetti, balsamic chicken, baked manicotti and Fabio fillet (served in a red wine and veal stock sauce). It is all outstanding, but don't overlook the baked lasagna. You can just know that it is as good as it gets.

The DiFabio menu features chicken and veal specialties.

26

Laura DiFabio, a pastry chef, makes all of the desserts in-house. The three layer cappuccino cheesecake, uptown strawberry shortcake, Italian cream cake, and key lime pies are some of the offerings. But it's the tiramisu and crème brulee that are the real crowd favorites.

The DiFabio's set out to open a very good Italian restaurant back in 1995. And guess what? They did!

Address:
17 West Center Street
Hours:
Open, 5:00 p.m. – 9:00 p.m., Wednesday – Saturday
Phone:
270/825-1900
Price Range: $$
Area Attractions:
Gov. Ruby Laffoon Log Cabin

27

Ferrell's Hamburgers

HOPKINSVILLE, KENTUCKY

Have you eaten at Ferrell's? It's a common question if you're passing through Hopkinsville and stop and ask where a good quick place is to eat.

The cozy little downtown diner with white counters and 16 green stools take up pretty much all of the dining area as the smell of hamburgers and onions permeate the air.

When at Ferrell's you're ready for a burger, and Cecil Doris Ferrel is usually there to make sure you get one, and if not one, maybe a whole bag of 'em. After all, they've been doing this since they opened for business in 1936.

Not many changes have been made over the years, especially when it comes to the menu. It's still mostly burgers, chili, pecan pie and soft drinks, and since the diner is open 24 hours a day, eggs, ham, sausage, bacon and toast are the order for breakfast.

Ferrell's lays claim to being the first Hopkinsville business to offer air conditioning. They say it was a good way for some of the nearby Ft. Campbell soldiers to cool off and have a meal in the early days.

"We have gotten and still get a lot of business from the soldiers," offers Mrs. Ferrell. "They buy 'em by the bag, 30 or 40 at a time."

Over the years a lot of famous people have dined at Ferrell's. They recall the time Guy Lombardo's band stopped in, and in more recent times the country music group, Sawyer Brown, spent some time getting their cheeseburger fix.

Address:
1001 Main Street
Hours:
24 hours a day, 7 days a week
Phone:
270/886-1445
Price Range: $
Area Attractions:
Bravard Winery

Hih Burger

MURRAY, KENTUCKY

Nothing fancy on the outside. In fact the sign standing between the street and Hih Burger's parking lot could probably use a new paint job. Nothing fancy on the inside either. Several booths, a counter with six stools, and several Formica-topped tables that seat about 80 and that's it. Well, not quite.

Almost anytime of the day Hih Burger is packed with customers. At lunch time there's usually a wait for one of the seats you hope will free up.

Owner Larry Roberson hasn't put a whole lot of emphasis on a frilly décor, but he has put an emphasis on carrying on a family tradition since 1957 of serving outstanding food.

"I'm not exactly sure where the name came from," says Roberson. "Mom and dad moved away for work in Detroit," he continued. "When they came back they modeled it after a restaurant they had seen there."

By all means you can get a burger at Hih Burger, but it's those breakfast offerings and incredible lunches with all of those home-style vegetables that really get your attention.

"We do everything we can from scratch," Roberson says. "We even boil our yams and then cook them in the oven. We don't even use a cake mix with our cakes."

Breakfast which begins at 5:00 a.m. consists of just about anything you want including omelets, pancakes, French toast, country ham and, oh, that milk gravy.

Lunch at Hih Burger is really special. Fish, Chicken and Dressing, Bar-b-Que, Roast Beef, Pork Chops, Chicken, Ham, Tenderloin, Pinto Beans, Lima Beans, Fried Corn, Fried Okra, Mashed Potatoes, Hush Puppies, two kinds of Slaw, cornbread, Broccoli Casserole and Hamburger Steak. The list goes on and on.

Daily specials are the norm at Hih burger, but the extensive menu gives customers a choice that no one will be disappointed in.

Hih Burger is not open for evening meals.

"We put so much energy into our breakfast and lunches that we don't do dinner," says Roberson.

DINERS INFORMATION

Address:
413 S. 4th Street
Hours:
Open, 5:00 a.m. – 2:00 p.m., Monday – Sunday
Phone:
270/753-1155
Price Range: $
Area Attractions:
Kentucky Lake
Murray State University

Hill's Bar-B-Que

MAYFIELD, KENTUCKY

It's a fourth generation restaurant that is still going strong after more than 50 years. So they must be doing something right. They are! They're serving up good food just the way it was done by owner Greg Hill's grandparents when it all began. And now Greg is in the process of passing the torch to son Jace and daughter Allison to continue the tradition.

The signature item is the hickory smoked bar-b-que, slow cooked just the way Greg's dad, Jerry, did it. Top it off with their one-of-a-kind sauce. Pour a little and you're okay. Add a touch more and you're still alright. But add some more and you better get ready to rumble. It's great!

A crowd favorite is the chili dog plate.

A customer said, "It's been several years since I've been back to Mayfield, but I had to come to Hill's and have the chili dog plate. It taste just like it did the last time."

Hill's has an extensive menu from fried dill pickle wedges, to bar-b-que ham, turkey, chicken, ribs, to white beans and cornbread, to burgers to steaks and chops, to salads, and of course to those homemade chocolate and coconut pies Greg's mom still makes.

The walls and ceiling at Hill's are covered with memorabilia that represents the local history of the entire area from pictures, to old high school letter jackets to stuff.

Hill's Bar-b-que has another claim to fame in the area. It had

the first drive through window with a speaker to order from.

"Some of the locals said it wouldn't work when my dad first tried it with an old speaker," recalled Greg. "But it did, and before long all of the other restaurants were trying to get one."

Over the years lots of people have eaten at Hills. One of the more famous was Jerry Seinfeld a few years ago. Supposedly he was in the area to look at a filming location.

"We didn't treat him any different than anyone else," says Hill. "We treat every customer like we'd like to be treated."

Address:
1002 Cuba Road
Hours:
Open, 11:00 a.m. — 10:00 p.m., Monday — Saturday
Closed Sunday
Phone:
270/247-9121
Price Range: $
Area Attractions:
Icehouse Art Gallery & Museum

Horseshoe Steakhouse

HOPKINSVILLE, KENTUCKY

This restaurant opened its doors in 1968 in a little building that once was a drive-in restaurant. Today the Horseshoe Steakhouse is still little, seating only 64, but they've been turning out some mighty good food ever since.

All of the food is prepared on a grill right behind a small bar with several stools. And these bar stools are always in demand by the locals.

"Many of our regular customers like to sit at the bar and watch their food being cooked," says Faye Allen, who has worked at the Horseshoe since 1974.

What you'll see on the grill is usually lots of steaks. The 32-ounce super sirloin for two and the 8-ounce filet are two of the most popular beef choices. But rib eyes, T-bones and strips find their way on a lot of plates as well.

Even though the Horseshoe is primarily known for its steaks, they do, indeed, serve other good food. Pork chops, country ham and Cajun chicken, as well as shrimp cocktail, potato skins and a large selection of fresh salads. Among the most popular sandwiches is their famous half-pound Horseshoe Burger. May I suggest a side order of their hash browns with no matter what you order? They're chopped on the grill with onions and paprika, and good is putting it mildly.

At the Horseshoe you'll see customers in a tux and some in work clothes. It's that kind of place. You'll also probably

see Dee working the grill like she has for the past 20 years. And Faye's sister Margie has also been there for over 20 years.

The restaurant has a full service bar.

DINERS INFORMATION

Address:
2112 Ft. Campbell Blvd.
Hours:
Open, 4:00 p.m. – 10:30 p.m., Monday – Thursday
4:00 p.m. – 11:00 p.m., Friday and Saturday
Closed Sunday
Phone:
270/886-7734
Price Range: $$
Area Attractions:
Trails of Tears Park

Hot Diggity Dog

CADIZ, KENTUCKY

Pat Boone's 1950's song "Hot Diggity Dog Diggity" was the inspiration for John Bryant to name his restaurant Hot Diggity Dog in Cadiz a few years ago.

As you might expect hot dogs are the specialties of the house. Not just any hot dogs mind you, but a Nathan's hot dog. Nathan's just might be the most famous and best hot dog in the world. You can't get them just anywhere, but you can in Cadiz.

"Word has gotten out that we sell Nathan's," says Bryant. "The tourist and retirees in the area know all about Nathan's New York hot dogs. It's a kosher dog and it's good."

Bryant started out with a hot dog cart and some time ago he was ready for a permanent location. His eatery, just off of the main drag, has several tables, a counter with six stools, a deck and tables for sidewalk dining.

As good as those huge chili dogs and Chicago style dogs, topped with tomato, cucumbers, virgin olive oil, sautéed onions and grey poupon mustard are, the restaurant serves other things they are proud of.

Tuna and chicken salad, kielbasa, corned beef, Reuben, and soups that include burgoo and potato bacon are also very popular items.

"We make most of our items from scratch," says Bryant. Our soups, cakes, pies and tuna and chicken salads are all made fresh."

Bar-b-que is a big seller at Hot Diggity Dog, and although Bryant doesn't fire up his own, he says what he serves is the very best he has tasted.

"We serve Knockum Hill from nearby Christian County, and everybody loves it," he adds.

Ice cream at Hot Diggity Dog is served in one of those big waffle cones. There's also another dessert that is off the charts. Death by Chocolate with O'Charley's caramel pie was described by one customer as a "don't leave here without it."

Address:
13 Marion Street
Hours:
Open, 10:00 a.m. – 4:00 p.m., Monday – Thursday
10:00 a.m. – 5:00 p.m., Friday and Saturday
Closed Sunday
Phone:
270/522-2258
Price Range: $
Area Attractions:
Lake Barkley

Ivy's Fine Dining

Sometimes the best food turns up in the most unexpected places. Like Hartford, Kentucky.

Ivy's Fine Dining in the center of town on Main Street offers up a menu that rivals many restaurants in much bigger towns.

Iris and Tim Johnson's restaurant seats approximately 100 customers in a combination of booths and tables. Although the outside of Ivy's is nothing fancy or even causes heads to turn when driving by, the inside is bright and cheery with lots of miniature white lights.

All of this is well and good, but not nearly as good as the food served up.

Lunch offers your typical noon-time fare: grilled chicken, French dip, fried catfish, stromboli, burgers, and a BLGT which is a BLT with a slight twist. It's bacon, lettuce and fried green tomatoes topped with ranch dressing on toast. But of all of the sandwiches, it's the Zak-Attack Burger (named after the Johnson's son) that is the king of all sandwiches. A full pound of Black Angus ground chuck on a huge gourmet bun is only for the very hungry.

The dinner offerings are top notch. It begins with an awesome homemade potato soup composed of big chunks of potatoes, real bacon bits, celery, a little cheese topping in a rich, creamy base. One customer was overheard tell-

ing a friend, "If you don't eat all of yours, I'll eat it."

A complete entrée selection of steaks, pork chops, delicious lightly breaded catfish, prime rib and baked spaghetti are very popular choices. But at Ivy's it's some of the real surprise side dishes and desserts that add to their delightful dining experiences.

The hot potato salad made with a bacon, honey-mustard dressing and bits of egg is a definite order. The homemade fries are seasoned just right, and as good as they are they go good with anything you order.

The unusual deep fried cheesecake is served in a bowl of vanilla bean ice cream and topped with your choice of chocolate, caramel or strawberry. You don't find this served everywhere.

DINERS INFORMATION

Address:
214 Main Street
Hours:
Open, 11:00 a.m. – 8:00 p.m., Monday – Thursday
11:00 a.m. – 9:00 p.m., Friday
3:00 p.m. – 9:00 p.m., Saturday
11:00 a.m. – 3:00 p.m., Sunday
Phone:
270/298-3838
Price Range: $$
Area Attractions:
Bill Monroe Birthplace

Kirchhoff's Bakery & Deli

Is it a bakery or is it a deli? Well it's both, and both are very good places to eat. All under the same roof in downtown Paducah, Kirchhoff's is considered somewhat a city tradition having been opened in 1873.

The bakery survived major floods in 1884, 1913 and 1937, but it didn't survive a terrible fire in 1952. After the bakery reopened five years later it closed for good when Louis Kirchhoff, Sr. retired. The building was no longer a bakery for the next 40 years until Louis, Jr. and his granddaughter Ginny reopened the business in 1997. As a fifth generation baker she still uses many of the original recipes of her great-great-great grandfather, Franz.

The deli side of Kirchhoff's is where most of the action is. Customers line up to place their order from a varied menu that includes, Reubens, pimento cheese, Italian eggplant, tuna melt and a fantastic Philly beef and cheese. They also feature a club, chicken and tuna salads. By the way, that club sandwich is not any ordinary club. Kirchhoff's is piled with herb roasted turkey, black forest ham, crisp bacon and cheddar topped with fresh greens, tomato and mayo on sourdough bread. They also have an assortment of salads and soups made fresh daily.

And now for the bakery side of Kirchhoff's.

They prepare everything

except doughnuts.

Those butterscotch brownies are . . . what is the saying ... to die for? There are also cookies, Danish, cakes, and pies.

As good as the lunch selections are, the same can be said about breakfast at Kirchhoff's. A pleasant surprise is the first rate gift shop right in the same building. Many of the items are one-of-a-kind.

DINERS INFORMATION

Address:
114-116-118 Market House Square
Hours:
7:00 a.m. – 5:00 p.m., weekdays
8:00 a.m. – 4:00 p.m., Saturday
Phone:
270/442-7117
Price Range: $
Area Attractions:
Quilt Museum, Flood Wall Murals, Tilghman Civil War Museum

Patti's 1800 Settlement

GRAND RIVERS, KENTUCKY

Patti's is a destination restaurant. Folks drive for a couple of hours just to eat here. Anyone who has ever been here knows, of course, about the pork chop. I don't mean just any pork chop either. The two inch thick chop is Patti's signature item. A close second is the eight inch "mile high" meringue pies. When waitresses set it down in front of you, it's almost like "this is a joke." No it's not a joke and neither is the rest of the food.

The homemade bread, served with a delicious strawberry butter, comes straight from the oven and overflows from the flower pot in which it is baked and served.

Everything on the menu is outstanding. When a restaurant serves over 250,000 meals a year, then you know it is good.

In the little town of Grand Rivers, population of 350, give or take a few, Patti's has evolved as a tourist attraction, and a good one at that.

What started out as a hamburger-ice cream shop in 1977, owned and operated by Bill and Patti Tullar and ably assisted by their children, has turned into a family operation that just keeps getting better and better with time.

Once you get to Patti's 1880 Settlement you quickly discover there's something to do here besides eat.

Behind the restaurant, is

the "settlement" area. This is a group of shops built to resemble an 1880 era. Here there is something for the entire family to do.

Not only shopping, but also a world-class miniature golf course, animal park, remote control boats, and for those who really want to take the plunge, a wedding chapel.

Patti's has established a reputation for their wonderland of lights display. For the Christmas Holidays over 500,000 lights are turned on making this a major attraction in western Kentucky.

DINERS INFORMATION

Address:
1759 J.H. O'Bryan Avenue
Hours:
10:30 a.m. — 9 p.m., Monday — Friday
10:30 a.m. — 10 p.m., Saturday
10:30 a.m. — 8 p.m., Sunday
Phone:
1-888/736-2515
Price Range: $$
Area Attractions:
Kentucky Lake, Lake Barkley

The Feed Mill Restaurant

Y ou don't have to travel to the bayou country of Louisiana to get some great Cajun style food. All you have to do is get to western Kentucky. Morganfield to be exact.

In 1997 the Wheatley family opened the Feed Mill Restaurant in an old cinder block building that once served as the Purina Feed Mill business. Today you wouldn't recognize what Malcolm, his wife Leslie, son Eddie who manages the restaurant, and all of the other Wheatley's have done to the place.

Much of the construction was done with cypress and poplar timbers from recycled barns in the area. The white oak flooring and old corrugated tin give the eatery the rustic look the Wheatley's wanted when they first started.

In the bar area, referred to as "The Roost", the walls are covered in a mural showing an old grist mill.

The Feed Mill can seat a whole bunch of people; 90 in the main room, 40 in the bar, and another 65 in their "Mardi Gras Room."

A large list of appetizers, including soups and salads, get you started with the Cajun theme. Gator tail, crawfish tail, shrimp, oysters on the half shell, gumbo and a Cajun popcorn salad are just a sampling.

Of course there's your standard fare of sandwiches. But it's the soft shell and catfish poboys that get your attention.

For the main course there's steaks and chops as well as a

selection of fried specialty dinners. Included in these offerings are softshell crab, gator tail, frog legs, crawfish, oysters, catfish and chicken. One item served here that probably no other restaurant in the book serves is the fried quail.

But what would a Cajun restaurant be without shrimp creole, red beans and rice, jambalaya, and crawfish etouffe'e? The Feed Mill serves it all.

This is a unique restaurant with unique food in a unique building and setting.

DINERS INFORMATION

Address:
3541 U.S. Hwy. 60E
Hours:
Open, 10:30 a.m. – 9:00 p.m., Monday – Thursday
10:30 a.m. – 10:00p.m., Friday and Saturday
Phone:
270/389-0047
Price Range: $
Area Attractions:
Camp Breckinridge Museum & Art Center

The Pelican Restaurant

LAKE CITY, KENTUCKY

Here's a suggestion. Don't go to the Pelican Restaurant unless you are hungry. When your order arrives at your table it's almost like there's been a mistake because of the amount of food.

If you catch a Saturday night prime rib special, be prepared to see the largest piece of beef ever placed before you. One serving is probably enough for three people.

The Pelican has been around since 1956, and is one of those eatery's that is open almost all of the time without being open 24 hours. Seven days a week their day begins at 5:30 a.m. They close at 10 p.m. Sunday through Thursday and 12 midnight Friday and Saturday.

Breakfast is a big deal here. It's served anytime the doors are open. Omelets, hot cakes, waffles, country ham, biscuits and milk gravy, sausage and bacon are all standard fare.

One couple who keeps a boat at one of the nearby lakes pointed out they eat at the Pelican every time they come here from their home in Indiana.

"We love the food here and there's plenty of it," they said.

The menu is loaded with sandwiches, lunch specials like roast beef, country fried steak, chicken tenders and fruit plate. There are all kinds of en-

trees such as jumbo gulf shrimp, breaded oysters, Cajun shrimp and scallops, chicken teriyaki, rib eyes, T-bones, chicken breast and spaghetti.

A lot of things are good at the Pelican, but the Creole catfish is exceptional. It's farm raised broiled filets that are dusted with Cajun spices and topped with peppers and onions. Oh, is it good!

For sandwiches try the patty melt. It's a hand-patted burger, covered with Swiss cheese and onions and served on grilled rye.

The restaurant also offers a soup and salad bar, usually with two soups to choose from. The desserts are homemade with strawberry pie available in season. The pecan pie is outstanding with each piece being big enough for two.

Nothing fancy at the Pelican including the food. It's just good and makes sure you will not leave hungry.

DINERS INFORMATION

Address:
Highway 62
Hours:
Open, Sunday – Thursday, 5:30 a.m. – 10:00 p.m.
Friday and Saturday, 5:30 a.m. – 12:00 midnight
Phone:
270/362-8610
Price Range: $$
Area Attractions:
Kentucky Lake

The Purple Onion

The Purple Onion in Central City could just as easily be called a "purple jewel" because it is indeed a jewel of a restaurant.

Sheila and Ron Brownlee have done a jewel of a job in bringing a first class eatery to an area that some of the locals say has been underserved.

The restaurant has a sophisticated look to it in a brick-walled building that formerly housed a furniture store. The partially exposed brick, globed candles, purple cloth napkins are a nice classy touch in a town that claims The Everly Brothers. And guess what they've got? A menu that goes along with the look.

There's usually a chalk board special that greets customers when they walk in the door. If the board touts the cheesy potato or vegetable soups, go for it. Luncheon favorites include the purple onion burger, beer battered fish, breaded deep fried shrimp, and an assortment of sandwiches that include chicken salad and hickory smoked bar-b-que. But it's the roast beef and provolone composed of thinly sliced beef stacked on a croissant with grilled onion and pepper topped with chipotle sauce that draws praise.

A couple of nice touches at the Purple Onion that do not go unnoticed are the warm plates on which hot food is served. And the bread of the day is honey-glazed rolls. The honey brushed on is just the right amount to make a difference.

But dinner is when the stars come out, and the stars here are the more than adequate menu selections.

It starts with shrimp jammers to blooming onions to quesadillas to five alarm chili on potato wedges.

Prime rib, rib eyes, bacon wrapped pork chops, lemon pepper salmon, chicken alfredo and seafood gumbo really shine bright when looking at the menu. An assortment of side items from corn on the cob, potato cakes and pasta salad add to the experience.

But the grand finale is the banana pudding. Yes sirree, this is not just any banana pudding. The pudding is topped with graham cracker crumbs that is topped with fresh banana slices!

DINERS INFORMATION

Address:
113 North 1st Street
Hours:
11:00 a.m. – 10:00 p.m., Monday – Thursday
11:00 a.m. – 12:00 p.m., Friday – Saturday
11:00 a.m. – 3:00 p.m., Sunday
Phone:
270/757-1193
Price Range: $
Area Attractions:
Lake Malone

Wolf's Restaurant & Tavern

HENDERSON, KENTUCKY

If you could draw up a plan to create the perfect restaurant and bar in a somewhat yesteryear setting where everybody knows your name, it would be Wolf's.

Located downtown at the corner of First and Green Streets in one of those shotgun style buildings, the "tavern" wasn't always a tavern. George Wolf opened his doors in 1878 as a bakery, and a few years later a saloon was added in the back room. In fact Wolf's claims to have been issued only the second liquor license in all of Kentucky.

The bakery was eventually dropped and over the years a restaurant evolved that compliments one of the outstanding local bars anywhere.

The Davis family, Tom, wife Debbie and dad Snoz run the show, and have done so since they purchased Wolf's in 1997.

"We're definitely a Cheers type bar," says Tom Davis. "But we continually work to offer a wider selection on our dinner menu."

As one might expect, there's lots of bar food here. Included is a hamburger that has been named best in Henderson for the last four years. There's also a fried bologna, polish sausage and corned beef. The thing they are really known for, since way back when, is the bean soup and cornbread. It's worth a trip to Wolf's just for this.

As popular as the bar area is, the "dining side" has become a great place to dine. Steaks, chops, hot browns (Wolf's style), shrimp, catfish and other special seafood offerings, make

the restaurant a great place to eat.

Of course there are other selections, too numerous to list, as well as special choices for children and seniors.

This is one of those historic taverns that has a fantastic atmosphere and serves up some pretty good eats.

DINERS INFORMATION

Address:
Corner of 1st and Green Street
Hours:
Open, 11:00 a.m. – 9 :00 p.m., Monday – Thursday
11:00 a.m. – 10:00 p.m., Friday and Saturday
Tavern only 11:00 a.m. until ??? Monday – Saturday
Phone:
270/826-5221
Price Range: $$
Area Attractions:
W.C. Handy Festival, Audubon Park

AROMA'S KOFFEE KOTTAGE	MT. STERLING, KY
ATOMIC CAFÉ	LEXINGTON, KY
BACK HOME RESTAURANT	ELIZABETHTOWN, KY
BEAUMONT INN	HARRODSBURG, KY
BUCK'S RESTAURANT AND BAR	LOUISVILLE, KY
THE CREAM STATION	NEW HAVEN. KY
THE DEPOT	GLENDALE, KY
DOE RUN INN	BRANDENBURG, KY
ENGINE HOUSE CAFE	WINCHESTER, KY
BOONE TAVERN HOTEL	BEREA, KY
THE GLITZ	NONESUCH, KY
HANNA'S ON LIME	LEXINGTON, KY
HENNING'S	LEBANON, KY
HOLLY HILL INN	MIDWAY, KY
ISAAC'S CAFE	CLERMONT, KY
KERN'S KORNER	LOUISVILLE, KY
KURTZ RESTAURANT	BARDSTOWN, KY
KRESO'S RESTAURANT	BARDSTOWN, KY
LOUIE'S RESTAURANT	PARIS, KY
MISSY'S OUT OF THE WAY CAFE	RAYWICK, KY
MORDECAI'S ON MAIN	SPRINGFIELD, KY
OLD STONE INN	SIMPSONVILLE, KY

CENTRAL REGION

Aroma's Koffee Kottage
MT. STERLING, KENTUCKY

"I sure wish we had a place like this in Charleston," the lady said to her friend across the high rise table. "I've traveled all over the country and this is one of my very favorite places to have lunch."

And so it is with Aroma's Koffee Kottage in downtown Mt. Sterling at 31 S. Maysville Street. The setting is in a 1905 building that has a history of being a farm equipment store, a clothing store, and antique shop until owner Glenda Richardson opened her unique restaurant and coffee house.

The first thing you notice is all of those blackboards. They are everywhere, and the printing on them is so neat that customers want to take the time to read all of them. Some are ten to twelve feet off the floor. That's where Glenda's taping-chalk-to-a-broom-handle technique comes in. That's how she prints those boards way up on the wall. No step ladders here.

Aroma's specializes in Italian Panini sandwiches, hand-rolled wrap sandwiches, soups, salads, gourmet coffee drinks, smoothies and desserts.

Breakfast is served anytime. Hawaiian pancakes, banana split waffles, southwestern scramble and omelet in a mug are just a few of your morning choices. And Italian Panini's are special, too. They are served on grilled ciabatti loaves with pickle and chips. The wraps are served inside a hand-rolled 12" tortilla and then grilled.

One of their

catchy wraps is called a Frank Sinatra Wrap; do it your way. Build your own wrap from Aroma's fresh ingredients.

And now for the really, really good stuff – those drinks!

Aroma's even has a special drink menu. There are well over a hundred drink combinations available from coffees, to lemonade freezes, ice tea freezes, low fat smoothies, Italian cream sodas, espressos, cappuccinos, hot ciders, health tonics (really!), milkshakes, ice cream floats, bananas foster, coffee float and even a peanut butter and jelly cappuccino.

At Aroma's you drink your dessert.

While there you can't help but take in the gift shop. For the most part you will be eating or drinking in it. Things and such all around are for sale. Take your time and enjoy.

DINERS INFORMATION

Address:
31 S. Maysville Street
Hours:
Open, Monday-Friday, 8:00 a.m. – 5:00 p.m.
 9:00 a.m. – 4:00 p.m., Saturday
Phone:
859/498-1133
Price Range: $
Things of interest:
Old Silo Golf Course

Atomic Café

LEXINGTON, KENTUCKY

"It makes me feel like I'm on vacation," exclaimed one customer as she walked into the Atomic Café.

Although the name of the restaurant may not exactly fit the Caribbean theme, it is one fine place to eat and have fun.

The hand painted murals on the walls and ceilings create an island feel with its palm trees, assorted species of fish and an almost life size old beach cabin directly behind the bar.

Inside seating accommodates 100, while the beautiful meandering patio outside can handle another 150 under festive lighting at night.

Owners, Dale Holland and Bill Riddle, have done an outstanding job in establishing an independent themed eatery in a city full of restaurants.

Atomic Café sits just across from Transylvania University at 265 N. Limestone Street at the corner of Third. There's adequate parking in a lot next to the restaurant. They've been around for some fourteen years and things just keep getting better and better, especially the menu.

Specials abound at the Atomic Café. How about this for an evening dinner? Coconut Crusted Tuna prepared with a pineapple soy sauce as an appetizer. For the salad Granny Smith Apples and Smoked Mozzarella with pecans, mixed greens and green apple dressing. For the main course your choice of Pan Seared Black Grouper over saffron rice with fiery red and sweet yellow pepper sauces, or Blackened 14 oz. T-Bone over Chipotle Yukon Gold

Mashed Potatoes with a Coconut Mustard Sauce. And you can put the finishing touches on it with Peanut Butter Bread and Caramel Sauce.

Sounds like a vacation after all! Just to prove it you'll want to choose from a variety of "frozen concoctions that help you hang on."

Other specialties include the chicken pot pie, black beans and rice, grilled rib-eye, jerk chicken, shrimp and chicken kabob, but it's the Ropa Vieja that is a must. It's a Latin-style pot roast stewed with a mixture of tomatoes, peppers, onions, capers, olives and celery over rice. It comes with sweet potato chips.

DINERS INFORMATION

Address:
265 N. Limestone Street
Open:
4:00 p.m. – 10:00 p.m., Tuesday – Thursday
4:00 p.m. – 11:00 p.m., Friday and Saturday
Closed Sunday and Monday
Phone:
859/254-1969
Price Range: $$
Area things of Interest:
Kentucky Horse Park, Horse Farms

Back Home Restaurant

ELIZABETHTOWN, KENTUCKY

Never let it be said you can never go back home. The Back Home Restaurant in E'town makes sure you can, and when you do, they make sure you have some good food to eat.

Located in an historic 1872 home in downtown, Linda and Tommy Fulkerson didn't plan on operating a full grown restaurant - - at least not in the beginning. It actually evolved through an antique and craft shop, with a sideline of a few customers snacking on some beans and cornbread, pimento cheese sandwiches and a piece of pie. All of a sudden the display space gave way to more hungry customers and soon Back Home was a full service restaurant.

The second floor of the old home still has a fantastic antique and gift shop.

Today, daughter Lori and husband Steve, pretty much run the operation, but dad still handles much of the kitchen chores while mom, Linda, keeps an eye out just to help.

Most of the early day family recipes are still being served, but the good thing is they've added a whole lot more.

The stuffed tomato with chicken salad or tuna is a crowd favorite as is the French dip. It's thinly sliced roast beef on a hoagie roll and a tasty au jus dip.

If it's a heartier appetite you want to please, Back Home can meet those needs too.

The open face roast beef, with real mashed potatoes, cov-

ered with rich brown gravy and a side vegetable, is a choice that will make you proud. The Back Home hot brown is a delightful combination of ham, turkey, cheese sauce, two big slices of bacon criss-crossed over a large tomato slice, and then oven baked.

Clifty Farm country ham, chicken, and country fried steak also highlight the menu. A choice of cobblers and a brownie supreme are great finishes to any meal at Back Home.

DINERS INFORMATION

Address:
251 West Dixie Avenue
Hours:
11:00 a.m. – 3:00 p.m., Sunday and Monday
11:00 a.m. – 9:00 p.m., Tuesday – Saturday
Phone:
270/769-2800
Price Range: $
Area Attractions:
Coca-Cola Museum, Ft. Knox

Beaumont Inn

HARRODSBURG, KENTUCKY

Years ago hospitality and travel guru Duncan Hines (yes, the same whose name is on boxes of cake mix) listed his favorite place to eat as The Beaumont Inn.

Today, Chuck and Helen Dedman, along with son Dixon, own and operate the historic inn that has been in the family for some 90 years.

Constructed in 1845 as a school for young ladies, today the Beaumont Inn reeks with genuine hospitality, just as it did years ago.

Upon entering the grounds of the inn, you will immediately know that you have arrived at someplace special.

A couple of years ago the Beaumont Inn added a delightful lower level tavern, called the Old Owl Tavern. It features a full service bar and a large wood burning fireplace that enhances the exposed brick walls and wood beamed ceiling.

But so much for the tavern.

The main dining room is what sets the Beaumont Inn apart. You feel as though you have stepped back into another era with gracious service and wonderful food.

You can pretty much bet that anything you order will be good, but if there's any doubt, order their very own two-year-old Kentucky cured country ham or the famous yellow-legged fried chicken. Both were favorites of Duncan's years ago. The Beaumont is also known for their corn pudding and orange lemon cake.

They also serve up what they

call the Hot Beaumont, a variation of a hot brown. It's made with roast pork loin, tomatoes on toast points and smothered in a delicious Dijon cream sauce.

Such Southern hospitality, on the 30 acre setting with 29 guest rooms, is a must visit even if you do nothing but eat and stroll the grounds.

I must confess that the Beaumont Inn is one of the exceptions to "out-of-the-way places to eat," that make up most of the unique restaurants in this book. It is, indeed, a destination restaurant that just happens to be my favorite place to visit.

DINERS INFORMATION

Address:
638 Beaumont Inn Drive
Hours:
Open, Wednesday-Saturday, lunch
Wednesday-Saturday, dinner
Sunday Brunch Buffet
Closed Monday and Tuesday. www.beaumontinn.com
Phone:
859/734-3381
Price Range: $$
Area Attractions:
Ft. Harrod, Shakertown

Buck's Restaurant and Bar

Located in the old Mayflower building in the historic St. James area of old Louisville this is one fine place to dine. Some places you eat, but at Buck's you dine!

A bar near the front is accented by masses of white flowers in clear crystal and cut glass vases. White flowers are everywhere, only adding to the elegant but comfortable setting.

The food, the atmosphere and the service, set Buck's apart and truly make a visit here an experience.

The live piano music and the hodgepodge of mismatched china offers a whisper to visitors to relax and enjoy.

Lunch at Buck's includes a hot brown, chicken stir-fry, crab cakes, beef stroganoff and a delightful pasta carbonara, which is country ham sautéed with garlic and olive oil, tossed with mushrooms and linguine and topped with a parmesan cream sauce.

But it's when darkness falls on the outside that the stars light up on the inside at Buck's, and proprietor Curtis Radar has done a magnificent job in continuing a great tradition.

Appetizers run from Maryland crab cakes to shrimp scampi, to oysters Rockefeller to mushroom ravioli. An assortment of salads is highlighted by the baked goat cheese salad. This is mixed greens, olives, red onions and a fruit atop the baked goat cheese.

The big show features some of the more traditional offerings such as steaks and chops. However,

it's a real compliment to the menu at Buck's with the rack of lamb, breast of duck, seafood Caribbean style, orange roughy and stuffed crab.

There are two dishes that you can get here that probably are not served anywhere else, at least in Kentucky. The crispy fish with hot sweet Chili is a white fish sautéed in sesame oil until crispy and then topped with bell peppers, red onions and a hot sweet chili sauce. And then there are the spicy Cantonese noodles with chicken. The menu advertises that "this dish is extremely spicy." Take a bite and blast-off.

Every dish is a picture in its presentation as is the entire restaurant, including even the rest room and Cigar Room for those who want to partake.

DINERS INFORMATION

Address:
425 W. Ormsby
Hours:
Lunch, 11:00 a.m. – 3:00 p.m., Monday – Friday
Dinner, 5:00 p.m. – 10:00 p.m., Monday – Thursday
5:00 p.m. – 11:00 p.m., Friday and Saturday
Phone:
502/637-5284
Price Range: $$$
Area Attractions:
Slugger Museum, Churchill Downs

The Cream Station

The Cream Station likes to say they are located at the corner of the first stop light in New Haven. You could just as easily say they're located at the last stop light as well. You see, there's only one light in town.

The built-sometime-in-the-1800s structure was a lot of things before it became the Cream Station. First it was a bank (they've got the huge walk-in safe to prove it), then it was a post office, and like many old buildings, it fell on hard times. A carpet store and even a tattoo shop called the building home for a while, before Bill and Gertrude Holton decided it was the perfect place for an ice cream shop.

Ice cream, shakes, malts, sundaes, and banana splits were the hook for the Cream Station, but it has been those "comfort" sandwiches and homemade soups and chili that have kept the locals coming back.

The restaurant has a little bit of a train theme in keeping with the Kentucky Railway Museum located across and down the street a bit. An electric train travels around the restaurant on a track located on a shelf a few feet below the tin covered ceiling. There, a giant mural of a train engine coming straight toward you when you walk into the giant safe.

The menu here is on the wall. You order and they prepare.

"Some people come in and get a little fussy, but we don't fix nothing until they order," says Pat from behind the counter.

The pork tenderloin and a bowl of either the chili, bean or potato soup makes for a heck of a meal. It also comes with a square of

cornbread. The potato soup has more than just potatoes. Celery, carrots, garlic, and onions give it a special touch.

Chili dogs, mule ear strips (chicken), chicken salad, fish and chicken sandwiches, and burgers round out the selections.

In addition to the ice cream, The Cream Station is known for its pies, cakes and candy.

DINERS INFORMATION

Address:
149 South Main
Hours:
Open, 10:00 a.m. — 9:00 p.m. daily; winter hours vary
Phone:
502/549-9333
Price Range: $
Area Attractions:
Kentucky Rail Museum

The Depot

GLENDALE, KENTUCKY

Don't let Exit 86 on I-65 at Glendale mislead you. It's your typical exit, a couple of truck stops and two or three gas stations. Stick with it, drive a couple of more miles and you will arrive at Glendale, a Kentucky antique mecca. And there it is, on your left, just before you cross the railroad tracks is The Depot Restaurant. You can't miss it. It is in an old depot.

Owner Tony York has brought a New England style bistro to this Hardin County community and it is outstanding.

You can't help but be impressed, even before the food arrives. White linens spill over the tables beneath a vase of fresh flowers, and if you're in the main dining area you can't help but notice the white grand piano.

York likes to vary his menus, usually depending on the time of year it is. His seafood creations go hand-in-hand with the usual Kentucky traditional dishes such as hot browns and country ham. Yes there are the usual sandwiches and salads, but it's the special preparation that goes into the Marcella's Grilled Salmon with Lobster Cream, or the Backfin Crab Cakes with white wine beurre blanc shrimp and sea scallops, or the Bacon Wrapped Filet Mignon and Cold Water Lobster Tail, or the pastas, or the raw bar, or the chowders. Oh, did I mention the Southern Fried chicken with milk gravy, butter-milk biscuits, green beans, new potatoes and fresh melon.

It's probably a good bet that those vegetables and fruits came from a nearby Glendale

farm. That's what Tony York likes to serve when they are in season.

The Depot is open every day except Christmas and does suggest you make reservations, although they are not required.

The slogan for The Depot is "fighting the corporate giants' one great meal at a time." You know, they may be making some headway.

DINERS INFORMATION

Address:
Highway 222
Hours:
Open, 9:00 a.m. – 9:00 p.m. daily
Phone:
270/369-6000
Price Range: $$
Area Attractions:
Antiques

Doe Run Inn

BRANDENBURG, KENTUCKY

For well over 60 years the Doe Run Inn near Brandenburg has been cooking foods and renting rooms for visitors to the old mill that dates back to 1790.

Today, Ken and Cherie Whitman operate Doe Run and their intent is to maintain the tradition of turning out good country cooking. Although the Inn has a warm, rustic feel, it also has a nice splash of class with the cloth tablecloths and napkins.

The Whitman's have some close ties to the restaurant and inn, of which there are nine rooms to rent. Cherie is the grand niece of Curtis and Lucille Brown who ran Doe Run from 1958 to 1983, and it was them who set the standard for good eating. Ken's mom was employed as a waitress at Doe Run for some 17 years, so both of the Whitman's have it engrained in them.

If you go on Sunday you'll get the buffet only. No menu service is offered. But what a buffet it is with 50 items to select from.

Friday night offers a seafood buffet in addition to the full menu.

As good as those buffets are, it's the menu items that really make the food at Doe Run Inn special.

It begins with those made-from-scratch salad dressings: blue cheese, ranch, 1,000 island and French. They are so good you could eat them with a spoon.

If you've got four or more in your group the food is served in bowls, family-style.

Some things to consider when you visit the Doe Run Inn are the country ham with red eye gravy and

68

biscuits. Or you may want to choose the blackened trout with hushpuppies. The trout is light and flakey served with an assortment of vegetables that include slow-cooked green beans, new potatoes, and possibly the best slaw you've ever eaten.

"We cook our green beans all day long," says Ken Whitman.

But the fried chicken with milk gravy is what really jumps out at you. When ordered off the menu it is prepared in a 200-year old cast iron skillet.

"Uncle Curtis said Col. Sanders came here once and told him that the chicken at Doe Run was actually better than his," said Ken.

Taste it and decide for yourself.

The finishing touch is the lemon chess pie with a hint of coconut.

"It's Aunt Lucille's forty year old recipe," adds Whitman with pride.

DINERS INFORMATION

Address:
500 Doe Run Inn
Hours:
Open, 8:00 a.m. – 8:00 p.m. All Year
Closed December 24 & 25
Phone:
270/422-2982
info@doeruninn.com
Price Range: $$
Area Attractions:
Otter Creek Park

Engine House Cafe

"You're getting ready to have a flash back," says Bob Tabor, owner of the Engine House Café, in referring to his beer cheese. "It's the old Johnny Allman's recipe."

Last year Bob sold 8,000 pounds of the spicy spread under the name of River Rat Beer Cheese.

The café is located in an 1885 old fire house with all kinds of engine house memorabilia scattered about. It's a friendly, casual setting with a 7-stool counter and several wooden booths around the wall. Nothing seems to match but everything seems to work. A wood burning pot belly stove anchors one corner in the rear, with a couple of tables around it.

Adding to the unique décor is a cast iron claw foot bath tub that has been converted into a couch. Nearby sits an old juke box that plays authentic background music.

The menu at the Engine House features a Hook 'n Ladder sub; a Kentucky Hot Brown with country ham, white cheddar cheese and a country mornay sauce (old fashioned gravy) and a hot ham hoagie. However, the real delight is Carl's pasta bar set up on

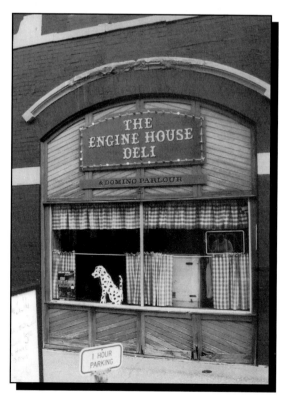

70

the counter prepared by chef cook Carl Coles. A visitor has a choice of the spaghetti or bow tie pasta alfredo sauce. An assortment of shakes and ice cream make the restaurant very kid friendly.

The Engine House has been a staple of downtown Winchester dining since 1984, and Bob Tabor, an old dinner theatre sort of guy lets his fire house theme and good food do his entertaining.

DINERS INFORMATION

Address:
9 W. Lexington Avenue
Hours:
Open, Monday, 11:00 a.m. – 2:00 p.m.
Tuesday-Friday, 11:00 a.m. – 4:00 p.m.
Friday Night, 5:00 p.m. – 9:00 p.m.
Phone:
859/737-0560
Price Range: $
Area Attractions:
Bluegrass Heritage Museum

Boone Tavern Hotel

BEREA, KENTUCKY

Built initially as a guest house for Berea College in 1909, Boone Tavern has grown from 25 original guest rooms to its current 58.

As charming as the rooms and beautifully appointed lobby are, much of the focus over the years has been directed to the hotel's restaurant.

It can be classified as a fine dining experience in a laid-back casual atmosphere. Although a coat and tie are not necessary, visitors will want to dress appropriately.

The restaurant has received international acclaim, with a menu that features a combination of traditional as well as creative southern cuisine.

The signature item at Boone Tavern is the Spoon Bread. Almost as soon as you are seated your waitperson arrives at your table and spoons you a serving. Don't worry they'll be back to bring you more. It is a cornbread-type mixture, light and fluffy enough for you to eat it with a spoon if you like. Not far behind the Spoon Bread is a favorite called Chicken Flakes In A Bird's Nest. It was created by a former innkeeper named Richard Hougen, who worked at Boone Tavern for more than three decades. This popular dish is a carefully prepared creamed chicken served on a crispy potato next to mashed potatoes, a vegetable and a tasty cranberry sauce.

Steaks, chops and various pork dishes dot the menu along with a fried green tomato salad topped with a unique sorghum mustard dressing. All kinds of other creative salads are available.

For those of you wanting only a sandwich, fear not. From burgers to catfish to chicken salad to an unusual mushroom burger, this restaurant has it.

A Sunday brunch transforms the hotel's lobby into a fairyland of omelets, French toast, steak and eggs, pancakes, hot browns, and quiche.

Over eighty percent of the wait staff in the restaurant is made up of Berea College students. All Berea College students work 10-15 hours per week in the College Labor Program. Students earn money for the books, room and board at the college, but do not pay tuition. There's more than a good chance your server here can tell you all about it.

If you stay in one of the guest rooms it will feature handcrafted cherry, oak or pine furniture made by students at the college over the past 100 years.

Boone Tavern is listed on the National Register of Historic Places.

DINERS INFORMATION

Address:
100 Main Street
Hours:
Breakfast 6 a.m. - 10 a.m., Monday – Sunday; Lunch 11:30 a.m. - 2:30 p.m., Monday – Saturday and Sunday 11 a.m. – 2:30 p.m.
Dinner 5:30 p.m. – 8 p.m., Monday - Sunday
Phone:
859/985-3702
Price Range: $$
Area Attractions:
Artisan Center, Arts and Craft shops

The Glitz

NONESUCH, KENTUCKY

The Glitz is an experience. Getting there is also an experience. The twisting, winding, two lane road begs you to slow down and enjoy the beautiful panoramic views of Woodford County's horse farms and rolling pastures. Just getting to the Glitz is half of the fun.

Located in the old Nonesuch Elementary School with it's stately façade, the Irish Acres Antique Gallery is what you see first when you walk through the front door.

Twinkling lights and sparkling chandeliers are everywhere. Every turn is a pleasant surprise. And this is just the antique portion.

At the end of the hall and down the steps, the real surprise awaits you. The Glitz.

You would never know you're in the basement's former school cafeteria. Talk about an extreme makeover. It has been transformed into an elegant, classy, yet somewhat gaudy dining room that just as easily could be located in Paris, New York City or San Francisco.

A set menu that changes bi-weekly awaits you. It includes a set price and includes the Glitz's signature spiced apple refresher drink, an appetizer, entrée, dessert and coffee and tea.

The Hannigan family, dad Arch and daughters Jane DeLauter and Emilee McCauley oversee the operations, and it's their attention to detail and the willing-ness to offer up a creative, imagi-native menu that is so much more than meat and potatoes.

Appetizers might include Irish potato soup, crabmeat cocktail or stuffed porta-

bella. Entrée selection could be halibut parmesan, chicken parisienne, pasta rotolo, or salmon en croute. Although the choice of desserts rotates, there's one that is always on the menu. The Nonesuch Kiss is the house special. A baked meringue shell filled with a scoop of jamoca ice cream, hot fudge sauce, toasted sliced almonds, whipped cream topped with a cherry makes this a must order.

DINERS INFORMATION

Address:
4205 Fords Mill Road
Open:
St. Patrick's Day through the last day of the year
Hours:
10:00 a.m. – 5:00 p.m., Tuesday – Saturday
Phone:
859/873-7235
Price Range: $$$
Area Attractions:
Horse Farms

Hanna's on Lime

LEXINGTON, KENTUCKY

Hanna's On Lime is not easy to find unless you're a local, and when you do you'll probably have to hunt for a parking space. There's no parking lot for Hanna's. It's a downtown restaurant in Lexington open for breakfast and lunch. Nothing fancy, mind you. Just as their slogan reads: "comfort food in a comfortable place."

With a green and yellow color scheme and fruit design plastic table-cloths, owner chef Beth Hanna has managed to build a cross section of business from downtown professionals, to families, to blue collar workers. The bottom line is the food is good.

Hanna, who played basketball and tennis at the University of Kentucky, has a few sports themed items on her menu. One in particular is the Micki D, named for the Wildcats lady basketball coach. It's a blackened cod fillet on a toasted bun with homemade tarter sauce, lettuce and sliced tomato served with fries.

A graduate of Sullivan School of Culinary, Hanna likes the opportunity to be creative with her daily specials and use of home grown ingredients from local farmer's markets. Daily specials range from meatloaf, chicken pot pie, salmon croquettes, spaghetti with meatballs, fried chicken, baked cod, and country fried steak.

Popular items are the pinto bean soup with corncakes, the veggie plate, the quiches and eggs benedict.

A lot of restaurants do pan-

cakes, but not many do them any better than Hanna's on Lime. They're big. Lot's of places have big pancakes, but they're not light and fluffy like Hanna's. She's got a special secret for your choice of blueberry, strawberry, banana or chocolate chip.

The menu offers other typical items you might expect: omelet's, country ham and biscuits, French toast, assortment of salads, burgers, B.L.T., Reuben, grilled marinated chicken, tuna and chicken salads.

Hanna's on Lime is worth a circle around the block a couple of times to catch a parking spot. If you're lucky you could get one of the three metered slots in front of the restaurant.

DINERS INFORMATION

Address:
214 South Limestone Street
Hours:
Open, Breakfast, 7:00 a.m. — 11:00 a.m.
Lunch, 11:00 a.m. — 2:00 p.m., Monday — Friday
8:00 a.m. — 12 p.m., Saturday
Phone:
859/252-6264
Price Range: $
Area Attractions:
Kentucky Horse Park/Horses

Henning's
LEBANON, KENTUCKY

When Monica and Michael Henning first opened their restaurant in downtown Lebanon back in 1993 they weren't really sure what personality it would evolve to. They had spent several months renovating the three-floor pre-Civil War building with a hope that the locals would come when they opened their doors.

Initially, they served up southern styled local food. It didn't take long for Henning's to evolve into a restaurant that not only satisfied the locals, but added menu items that also attracted "outsiders" to eat with them.

The Henning's take pride in that at least 90% of their menu offerings are made from scratch. Customers have quite a bit to choose from. Among the selections are hand cut steaks that, according to Michael Henning, customers can order cut to their specifications.

Friday night at Henning's is special. It's prime rib night. Customers from the surrounding communities drive in, and along with the locals, make it one very busy restaurant.

Henning's, of course still offers the southern traditional comfort foods that you might expect at a good eatery, among them fried chicken and country ham. An assortment of seafood entrees takes the spotlight. Dinners have their choice of the king crab legs, lobster tail and frog legs, as well as shrimp, salmon, sea scallops and rainbow trout. Rib eyes, T-bones, strips and a blue ribbon filet are the beef features that Henning's take pride in.

"We serve as good of beef as you can get anywhere," says Michael Henning. "And another thing we are going to try to do is raise some of our own produce. This way we can assure quality."

DINERS INFORMATION

Address:
157-159 Main Street
Hours:
Open, 4:30 p.m. – 9:00 p.m., Tuesday – Thursday
4:30 p.m. – 10:00 p.m., Friday and Saturday
Closed Sunday & Monday
Phone:
270/692-6843
Price Range: $$
Area Attractions:
Civil War History

Holly Hill Inn

MIDWAY, KENTUCKY

Once you are seated, you immediately know Holly Hill Inn is no ordinary restaurant. Patties of soft butter served on small porcelain plates with individual butter knives let you know this 1845 Greek Revival mansion is special.

From the white table cloths to the elegant napkin rings to the Victorian artwork on the walls, an informed, soft-spoken wait staff makes you feel as though they really are glad you are there.

Chris and Ouita Michael are the owners and chef. They provide visitors with a choice of menus that change monthly and feature traditional southern, American southwest and other continental cuisines. Customers can choose three, four or five course selections.

The atmosphere is one of quiet conversations in a relaxed atmosphere with just the right amount of background music. A very small full service bar with just enough room for two or three couples to wait for a table sits near the back of the house.

Some appetizers you may see, depending on when you visit, are Roquefort cheese cake with a walnut crust and Asian pear salad, or the breast of Kentucky squab. This is a green papaya salad and tangy vinegar syrup. But one of the favorites is the golden butternut squash bisque.

Now keep in mind that the lunch and dinner menus

are different. The dinner menu will usually offer a choice of fish and pasta or meat and fowl, whereas the luncheon choices range from chicken and dumplings to slow cooked beef estouffade. But it is those crispy Baltimore crab and shrimp cakes that steal the show. They are served with a mustard side. This alone makes your trip to Holly Hill worthwhile.

Of course there's a wonderful dessert menu that comes with the meal.

Restrooms are not usually talked about in dining books, but the ones here are nice enough to deserve a mention.

Reservations are recommended due to limited seating.

DINERS INFORMATION

Address:
426 North Winter Street
Hours:
11:30 a.m. – 2:00 p.m., Wednesday – Saturday
Dinner, Wednesday – Saturday, 5:30 p.m. until ?
Sunday Brunch, 11:30 a.m. – 2:30 p.m.
Phone:
859/846-4732
Price Range: $$$
Area Attractions:
Equus Run Vineyards

Isaac's Cafe

CLERMONT, KENTUCKY

A trip to Bernheim Forest in Bullit County, not far from Shepherds-ville, provides visitors with an experience of scenic beauty that rivals many woodsy type places in the United States. But now there's another reason to visit.

Isaac's Café, named for Isaac Bernheim, serves up lunch in the new visitors center in a setting that gives you a feeling of eating in the outdoors when you're actually inside.

"Because of where we are," I like to keep our menu selection as fresh as possible," says owner Rebecca Fulner. "I've taken some of my old family recipes and added my touch here and there to present a well rounded selection."

Rebecca's specialties are the Grilled Salmon. She also serves up a Salmon Burger. It's fresh salmon mixed with fresh red, yellow and green peppers, red onion and an array of spices. She serves it on fresh baked sourdough bread, topped with a garden goddess sauce.

Other offerings include the Gourmet Grilled Cheese, Grilled Chicken, German Reuben, Turkey Club, Tuna Melt and Veggie Wrap.

An Asparagus Salad can be or-dered in a full or half size. Tuna and Chicken Salad are very popular at Isaac's.

One of the items is labeled as Kristin and Trey's Favorite. It's supposed to be for kids, but kids of all ages order it, and who can blame them. After all, its toasted whole wheat topped with peanut butter and then covered with chocolate raisins. A side of fruit comes with it.

There's an entire panel on the

menu with a variety of sandwiches. Included are BLT's, Corn Beef, Chili Dog, Benedictine, Pimento Cheese and even a Soy Nutbutter and Preserves on Honey.

Just about everything at Isaac's can be made into a wrap, if that is to your liking.

To further prove the environmentally friendly personality of Bernheim Forest, the parking lot has two electric plugs for those visitors needing to re-charge their car.

Don't leave the grounds without driving through the well-marked forest. It is commonplace to see people out of their cars taking a closer look at trees or flowers, and often taking pictures. On occasion, artist will be perched on a rock, painting or sketching various vistas throughout the grounds.

DINERS INFORMATION

Address:
Bernheim Forest, Hwy 245
Hours:
Hours: Daily, 11 a.m. – 4 p.m.
Closed Tuesday
Phone:
502/543-3966
Price Range: $
Area Attractions:
Jim Beam Bourbon, Bernheim Forest, Hawk's View Galleries

83

Kern's Korner

If you're not familiar with the area, you can drive right past Kern's Korner at the corner of Bardstown Road and Lakeside Drive in what is referred to as the upper Highlands area. If you do miss it, by all means turn around or else you'll also miss the greatest cheeseburger ever! I'm not kidding. There may be some out there as good, but not better.

Kern's Korner being called a restaurant might be a stretch. It's a tavern that serves sandwiches. The sign says so, and it's the closest thing to a cheers bar that you'll find in Kentucky. Everybody knows your name. If they don't, they soon will.

Bobby Kern's owns the place. He bought it from his dad Bob, Sr. 16 years ago. Senior had run it for 13 years before that so it's been a neighborhood stopover for some 30 years with the Kern's name on it.

"My brother Jeff runs the operation," says Bobby, "and we use my mom's chili recipe."

That chili recipe is the second most popular on the menu, behind the cheeseburgers, of course.

"We serve pub grub," explains Bobby Kerns. "We also have chicken salad, tuna, turkey, roast beef, homemade soups, vegetable, bean and chicken noodle. But 90% of our sales are the burgers and chili."

Kern's Korner might come off as a sports bar, but to be more descriptive it is a horse racing bar. Lots of pictures of horses on the wall that are next to a picture of Louisville football great Paul Hornung.

Spyder, that's his nickname,

works the bar, and Margaret works the grill. They've been there for years. No one will take your order at one of the six high-top tables. You'll have to follow the instruction of a big sign on the wall that reads "Please Place Order at Bar." There are also some 20 stools at the bar for eating and tables on the patio that fronts Bardstown Road. The same rules apply to everyone, even if you are D. Wayne Lukas, Bob Baffert or one of the many other trainers or jockeys who frequent Kern's. And if you want to make a phone call, you'd better have a cell or 25 cents for the pay phone at the end of the bar. It's the only phone in the house.

"I don't have to look at a clock to tell what time it is," adds Kern's, "I can tell what time it is by who I see walking in the door."

Kern's has great atmosphere. Maybe it's not where you want to take the kids, but it is definitely where you want to go for the greatest cheeseburger ever and a cold one. Don't pass it up!

DINERS INFORMATION

Address:
2600 Bardstown Road
Hours:
Open, 9:00 a.m. til midnight daily
Phone:
502/456-9726
Price Range: $
Area Attractions:
Museums, Churchill Downs, Kentucky Derby

Kreso's Restaurant

BARDSTOWN, KENTUCKY

Dzevad and Merima Kreso once owned one of the best restaurants in all of Bosnia. That was before the war. Now they own one of the best restaurants in all of Kentucky. That's saying something because this state has plenty of outstanding places to eat.

Kreso's, located right in the middle of downtown Bardstown on N. Third Street, is an upscale eatery that has the feel of a "big city" restaurant. It's classy, with a movie house theme that carries over what the original building used to be. In fact the Kreso's have converted two old theaters into their restaurant even utilizing the balcony as a part of it. The large mural on the wall depicting Elvis Presley, Humphrey Bogart, Marilyn Monroe and James Dean sets the mood. A beautiful bar area with table dining, and an elegant dining room let you know this is a special place. The white table cloths and napkins, stemmed glassware, and heavy eating utensils only add to the ambiance as does the beautiful art collection hugging the walls.

The Kreso's are hands on owners, Merima in the kitchen and Dzevad is everywhere as he greets customers and works the bar and kitchen when needed.

Kreso's is quite international when it comes to menu choices: German, Bosnian, Hungarian, Italian and American.

"Our recipes are made from scratch" says Dzevad. "Everything is homemade. We create our own dishes that are not from a measured recipe."

The Kreso family has worked hard to create a friendly atmosphere.

"We want to do more than just take your order and prepare your food," offers Dzevad. "We want to make you feel at home here."

DINERS INFORMATION

Address:
218 North Third Street
Hours:
Open, 11:00 a.m. – 10:00 p.m., Monday – Saturday
11:00 a.m. – 9:00 p.m., Sunday
Phone:
502/348-9594
Price Range: $$
Areas of Interest:
Stephen Foster Amphitheatre

87

Kurtz Restaurant

BARDSTOWN, KENTUCKY

The beautiful two story stone Kurtz structure could favorably grace a magazine cover and not be out of place as it sits gracefully across the street from another well known "Kentucky Home," Federal Hill.

Marilyn Kurtz Dick, whose parents opened their home as a restaurant back in 1937, owns and operates the restaurant. It has always been a family endeavor first with mom and dad, then the children and now Marilyn's children and grandchildren.

Kurtz serves up delicious traditional southern food in a classy, warm atmosphere that exudes the feeling of dining in a beautiful home furnished in classic antiques. But as nice as the surroundings are, it's the food you are there for.

The skillet fried chicken, mashed potatoes and milk gravy have been a mainstay of Kurtz's just about as long as they have been open, and not far behind is the fried country ham with baked apples and red-eye gravy. The homemade soups and made-from-scratch casseroles are crowd favorites as are the pies, cobblers and biscuit puddings offered on the dessert list. But here is a suggestion when you go to Kurtz's: no matter what you order, make sure you ask for a serving of the skillet fried cornbread.

The lunch menu offers a selection of salads as well as several sandwiches to choose from. The Kentucky hot brown and hot roast beef sandwich, grilled pork loin, and fillet of cod round out a very solid luncheon menu.

Kurtz's has a selection of hand cut steaks from rib eye to strips to T-bone. Or customers can choose the roasted turkey breast, baked ham, chicken livers or top round roast beef. It's all good!

DINERS INFORMATION

Address:
418 E. Stephen Foster Avenue
Hours:
11:00 a.m. – 9:00 p.m., Tuesday – Saturday
12:00 noon – 8:00 p.m., Sunday
Closed Monday
Phone:
1/800-732-2384
Price Range: $$
Area Attractions:
Stephen Foster Amphitheatre

89

Louie's Restaurant

PARIS, KENTUCKY

Have no doubt about it, Louie's Restaurant in Paris is a horseman's establishment. Opened in 1984, it hits you right in the face when you pull up to the restaurant that sits on the corner at Tenth and Pleasant downtown.

The outside of the building, on two sides is decorated with wooden cutouts of jockey silks in an assortment of colors that represent some of the many horse farms in Bourbon County and the area. Bourbon County residents are quick to point out that nearby Fayette and Woodford counties don't have a lock on the thoroughbred business.

A quick glance at Louie's menu and you will know they are serious about this horse racing stuff. One heading is called the Furlong Sandwiches, and this is a list for a host of breakfast sandwiches: bacon, egg and cheese on bun, ham and egg on bun, country ham on bun, sausage and egg biscuit. Then there's the Home Stretch Breakfast that includes rib eye steaks, country ham, pork tenderloin and breakfast burrito. Other headings include the Quarter Pole, Fast Track, Morning Line and Near Side.

Louie's lunch menu continues the theme with headings called The Starting Gate, The Turf Course, The Back Stretch, The First Turn, The Watering Trough, and The Classic. In the last group you'll be able to select from Hot Roast Beef with thick brown gravy and a hearty serving of mashed potatoes. There's also a Rib eye Steak. But it's the Fried Chicken that Louie puts his name on. It's two pieces of

chicken breast that's guaranteed to be crispy on the outside and juicy on the inside. A side item comes with it.

The dinner menu continues with the Gulf Stream Specials featuring a selection of seafood. Another section is called the Yearling Feed and another, Across The Board. Here you have Italian Spaghetti with Meat Balls, Oriental Stir Fry, Brazilian Chicken and the Chicago Steak.

You'll want to get your order in quickly so you can walk around the dining room and check out the pictures hanging on the wall.

Depending on when you visit Louie's, you could see the likes of Seth and Arthur Hancock, D. Wayne Lukas, Kevin Costner, Randy Travis, Bob Baffert, Keanu Reeves, Toby McGuire, Rick Pitino or Tubby Smith.

DINERS INFORMATION

Address:
1000 Pleasant Street
Hours:
Open, 6:00 a.m. – 2:00 p.m., Monday – Saturday
5:00 p.m. – 9:00 p.m., Wednesday – Saturday
Closed Sunday
Phone:
859/987-6116
Price Range: $
Area Attractions:
Horse Farms

Missy's Out of the Way Cafe

RAYWICK, KENTUCKY

No one said finding Missy's would be easy, so here's my advice: When you think you're lost you haven't gone far enough; when you're sure you're lost, you're almost there.

For sure it is named appropriately, but, man oh man is it worth the hunt, and probably even a short wait, depending on the time you visit.

The parking lot at Missy's is shared by lots of pick-up trucks, a clunker or two and several SUVs, BMWs and maybe a Mercedes. Everything goes here and your John Deere hat will not be out of place.

Missy Luckett opened her restaurant here because it's where her dad had the land. Build it and they will come! But only if the food is good!

Missy has lots of things on her menu, but let's start with her Steak Nicole, named after her daughter. With that said, you know it's got to be good. The marinade is what separates this steak from all of the others, Missy will tell you. But what she won't tell you is the secret recipe. I will tell you the steak is big and the steak is good.

When you go to Missy's forget the diet, at least for this visit. With whatever you order you've got to try the S.O.B. fries. Missy actually created this specialty by accident.

"I didn't want to throw away a few of the leftover baked potatoes," she said. "So I came up with our south of the border potatoes."

The S.O.B.'s are a meal, topped with Cajun spices, onions, peppers, cheese, sour cream and bacon bits.

After you've done the main course, including an appetizer, I will tell you there probably won't be room for dessert. But just in case, just in case you do, you've got two great choices that I suggest.

The Mardi Gras Bar is a deep fried Snicker bar with almonds, topped with lots of unbelievable sweet stuff. The other selection is New York Cheesecake. At first glance the words New York might seem totally out of place at Missy's, but she makes it work. The cheese cake is outstanding.

Perhaps the understatement at Missy's is that everything seems out of place when it comes to the décor. Very few of the chairs match. Some are wooden, plastic and metal. Several naugahyde covered booths are present, and the small rips and tears only add to the ambiance. Another thing for sure is that Missy and her family doesn't throw anything away. They hang it on the wall or from the ceiling. You name it and its there: Life size posters, pool and beach toys, children's toys, and even a few watchmacallits.

Missy's offers a bar that serves beer and wine only. She's open Wednesday through Saturday only, and is known for taking a few days off during the summer. Make sure you call before you go.

DINERS INFORMATION

Address:
880 Horseshoe Bend Road
Hours:
Open, 5:00 p.m. – 9:30 p.m., Wednesday and Thursday
5:00 p.m. – 10:00 p.m., Friday
4:30 p.m. – 10:00 p.m., Saturday
Phone:
270/692-4892
Price Range: $$
Area Attractions:
Makers Mark Distillery

Mordecai's On Main

SPRINGFIELD, KENTUCKY

Downtown Springfield, with its refurbished store fronts and clean streets, is like many small towns in Kentucky in that it is trying to keep as much business in its historic district as possible. One of the big draws is Mordecai's Restaurant.

Named after Abraham Lincoln's dad, Mordecai Lincoln, the 200 seat restaurant is located in an old IGA grocery. But you would never know it unless you read it here. The brick front patio only gives a hint of what is on the inside.

Owners Greg Simms and Keith Schlosser have turned the location into one of the town's real jewels. People are enjoying the well-appointed décor with interesting framed photos, and dining areas that have been divided up so as not to look to open, but at the same time let customers see what's going on. A bar area occupies one side, yet doesn't dominate.

But it's the food that people drive here for says Keith Schlosser.

"Our customers come here from several counties away," he says "and that means they must like what we serve."

What they serve is a lunch and dinner menu that ranges from burgers, nachos, catfish and hot browns to steaks, ribs, chops, oysters, pasta, and honey bourbon salmon.

The big draw, though, is the Friday and Saturday night buffets, and the Sunday brunch. Prime rib night is big, and so are the fresh daily soups.

"We rotate some 20 different soups," says Schlosser.

Among the favorites are the 7-pepper, country bean, and the V.O.B. chicken and rice.

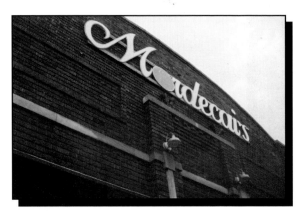

Oh, by the way V.O.B. is short for Very Old Barton.

The Sunday brunch features made-to-order-omelets and fantastic French toast, mashed potatoes and gravy, fresh vegetables, and fried chicken that is so good and moist that you'll swear it was prepared in a skillet.

Mordecai's a pleasant surprise, well worth a visit, and then another one and another. Its stylish simplicity and very good food make for a combination that equals a nice experience.

DINERS INFORMATION

Address:
105 W. Main Street
Hours:
11:00 a.m. – 9:00 p.m., Tuesday – Thursday
11:00 a.m. – 10:00 p.m., Friday and Saturday
10:00 a.m. – 2:00 p.m., Sunday
Closed Monday
Phone:
859/336-3500
Price Range: $$
Area Attractions:
Lincoln Homestead State Park

Old Stone Inn

SIMPSONVILLE, KENTUCKY

There's history here. There's also some absolutely wonderful food. The Old Stone Inn is a National Historic Landmark structure, built in the late 1700s. It's been a tavern, stagecoach stop, residence, inn, and since the 1920s, a restaurant. It's guest have included President Andrew Jackson and Revolutionary War General Marquis de Lafayette, so you better believe the food has got to be up to speed to keep up with the history. Proprietors Paul and Sally Crump have done a nice job in achieving this.

It has been said that the tone of a meal is set by the bread that is served. This certainly is the case at Old Stone Inn. The light, fluffy biscuits served with soft butter are indeed tone-setters.

This restaurant is one of those "don't-be-in-a-hurry" types. Relax and enjoy the moment. The service is top-notch. When a plate is empty it is almost immediately removed from your table.

Perhaps it would not be to far off to describe Old Stone Inn as country-gourmet dining. The white tablecloths and napkins, exposed stone walls, and uniformed wait staff add a classy touch to the dining experience.

All of this, however, would go for naught if the food didn't live up to everything else. It does!

The bourbon barrel pork chops with an apple cider glaze served with baked Weisenberger white cheddar grits are top shelf.

An array of choices include the braised beef short ribs, shrimp and grits, beef tenderloin, grilled salmon and steak are among a

96

fantastic list of other entrees as well as appetizers and salads. It is, however, a simple, delicious fried chicken dinner that receives high praise. The accompanying dishes of real mashed potatoes with milk gravy and the best southern style green beans you've ever tasted are surely what Old Hickory Andy ate when he visited. The green beans are prepared in a beef stock, with added bacon and a touch of onion.

A rock solid list of after dinner bourbons, single malt scotch, cognac and liqueurs make sure the evening ends just right. By the way, every Thursday is half price bottle of wine night.

DINERS INFORMATION

Address:
6905 Shelbyville Road
Hours:
Dinner, Tuesday – Saturday, 5:00 p.m. – 10:00 p.m.
Sunday Brunch, 10:30 a.m. – 2:30 p.m.
Phone:
502/722-8200 or 866/494-5683
Price Range: $$$
Area Attractions:
Horse Farm Tours

Our Best Restaurant

SMITHFIELD, KENTUCKY

This is the real thing! Our Best Restaurant is an authentic country store/restaurant, not one built and made to look like one. There must be at least 10,000 business cards attached to the walls, and an old barber's chair occupies one corner while an antique safe on four sturdy legs sits near the front door. "That's about as far as we could get it," says Kenny Way owner and manager of Our Best.

The restaurant sits across the road from a turn of the century mill that houses the Sack Room, a gift and antique shop run by Kenny's step-mother, Kay.

Kenny moves about the restaurant with an easy smile greeting regulars and introducing himself to the new ones, and is proud of the fact that son Aric is following him in the business.

There are two reasons not to come to Our Best; if you're not hungry or on a diet.

As you might expect the fried green tomatoes are delicious. What you might not expect is how awesome the fried cornbread is. The cornbread is great with everything on the menu, including the bean soup, pork chops, fried chicken, country ham, and, of course, the vegetable plate.

The side dishes at Our Best is like a who's-who of vegetables. Chilled pickled beets, green beans, corn, beans, fried apples, applesauce, mashed potatoes, kale, pinto beans and great northern beans are some that customers can select from.

The folks at Our Best will gladly tell you how to prepare the fried cornbread, but they will have nothing to do with giving you the

recipe for the most unbelievable peanut butter pie you've ever tasted. "If we tell you, we'll have to kill you." Kenny Way jokes. He also notes that Our Best cuts their pies in sixths not eighths.

On any given day the village of Smithfield, population 150, doubles or triples its numbers because of all the customers at Our Best.

DINERS INFORMATION

Address:
Giltner Road
Hours:
Breakfast, Saturday – Sunday only, 8:00 a.m. – 11:00 a.m.
Lunch and Dinner, Tuesday, Wednesday, Thursday and Sunday, 11:00 a.m.– 8:00 p.m.
Friday and Saturday, 11:00 a.m. – 9:00 p.m.
Phone:
502/845-7682
Price Range: $
Area Attractions:
Smith-Berry Winery

Papa Leno's

BEREA, KENTUCKY

One national publication listed Papa Leno's as a "Top 100 Independent Pizza Restaurants in America." And just think it's right there in beautiful, little ole Berea.

Back in 1984 the restaurant was opened in the downtown by Richard Bellando and named for his papa who happened to be called Leno. There you have it - - Papa Leno's.

Today the recipes are still the same and the Lewis brothers, Jerome and Brad, pride themselves in the "made-fresh-everyday" sauces and breads.

Pizza, naturally is big at this eatery. They like to say there's no guide lines as to what goes on a pizza at Papa Leno's. Each one is made fresh to the order right in front of you as the homemade dough is hand tossed until ready to spread. Sauces, seasonings, mozzarella cheese, along with your choice of toppings, result in a delicious pizza.

Papa Leno's is one of those order-from-the-counter and they-bring-it-to-your-table places. It's important to know that this restaurant is much more than pizza. Spaghetti, fettuccini Alfredo, lasagna, manicotti and chicken dishes are very popular choices among the locals. But if this is not to your choosing, how about soups, grilled chicken salad, stuffed tomato with chicken or tuna salad, buffalo wings and toasted cheese sticks. There's also an assortment of hot and cold sandwiches.

Papa Leno's offers a special "spaghetti night" every Tuesday night with special prices.

This is one of those great atmosphere restaurants where you'll find a mix of the local residents and college students that have one thing in common - - enjoying great food!

DINERS INFORMATION

Address:
108 Center Street
Hours:
Open, 11:00 a.m. — 10:00 p.m., Monday — Thursday
11:00 a.m. — 11:00 p.m., Friday and Saturday
12:00 noon — 10:00 p.m., Sunday
Phone:
859/986-4497
Price Range: $
Area Attractions:
Arts & Crafts

Paula's Hot Biscuit

HODGENVILLE, KENTUCKY

The town of Hodgenville, the birthplace of Abraham Lincoln, is not exactly on the main drag of Kentucky highways. So when Paula Varney opened her restaurant eight and a half years ago on one of the town's side streets, her family and friends said she had made a mistake and that she needed to be nearer to Lincoln's statue right in the middle of the square. Not!

"If you got good food they'll find you," she said. "And they did."

Paula likes to cook and her day of doing it usually begins around 4:30 a.m. each morning to get her Hot Biscuit open when the folks start coming in at 5 a.m.

Paula's Hot Biscuit doesn't offer a menu. You look over a chalk board that changes twice a day and place your order at an opening into the kitchen for breakfast and lunch.

"I've always loved to cook and the kitchen was the hub of our family life. We all gather around the kitchen," she explains. "I just love it."

Her customers are like family, too. One of them said she eats there twice a day because the food is good and she likes the people.

Another one, who was pedaling his bike across country from Battle Creek, MI., said he stopped in for the yummy food and to fuel his legs. "Always good food," he said.

The unpretentious eatery that once housed a building supply store has been recognized

recently by the Kentucky Pork Producers as their Restaurant of the Year, and once you taste the country ham, sausage and roast pork tenderloin you can see why. Of course those biscuits better be good, and they are.

Paula serves up some knee slapping lunch casseroles in the form of spaghetti, chicken and dressing, and squash. Along with casserole specials, Paula serves homemade soups with cornbread. Soups include potato (a speciality), chili, pinto bean, vegetable, and chicken noodle. A different plate lunch is served up daily as well.

"I sell a wash tub of those squash casseroles when I do them," she offered.

Don't judge Paula's Hot Biscuit by its out-of-the way location, the plastic table covers or the gum ball machine sitting near the door. Judge it by the great food you'll eat.

DINERS INFORMATION

Address:
311 W. Water Street
Hours:
Open, 5:00 a.m. – 10:00 a.m., breakfast
11:00 a.m. – 1:30 p.m., lunch, Monday through Friday
5:00 a.m. – 11:00 a.m., Saturday
Phone:
270/358-2237
Price Range: $
Area Attractions:
Abraham Lincoln Birthplace

103

Penn's General Store

GRAVEL SWITCH, KENTUCKY

Penn's General Store's location over the years has created some confusion for owner Jeanne Penn Lane, even though the store has been in the same family since 1850.

You see, their mailing address is in Marion County, they pay their phone bill in Casey County and their taxes in Boyle County.

Penn's is a you've-got-to-see-it store. The sagging floors, uneven ceiling, hand-worn counters makes it an education stopover, even if you don't want to eat a bologna or ham sandwich.

But please be advised you are not going to Penn's for the food. You're going there because there may not be anything else like it in America. You can do what generations of locals have been doing for a very long time, sitting around a Warm Morning Model 521 pot belly stove in a straight back chair enjoying a sandwich and drinking a bottle of pop. If you're so inclined you can even do a little shopping. The store's shelves are lined with all kinds of household goods and canned food items, from Clorox

to Tide soap, to coffee, tea and jars of stick candy.

For certain Penn's Store is an American original in that it is the nation's oldest store in continuous ownership and operation by the same family.

Remember, it's not the food you're coming here for.

DINERS INFORMATION

Address:
257 Penn's Store Road (just off Hwy. 243)
Hours:
Call ahead. Open only when Jeanne is there!
Phone:
859/332-7715 or 859/332-7706
Price Range: $
Area Attractions:
Pioneer Playhouse Theater

Rick's White Light Diner

FRANKFORT, KENTUCKY

If you've never been to Rick's White Light Diner drive real slow or you might miss it. It's only a few feet from the "singing bridge" on the opposite side of the main downtown area.

The small building has been a restaurant in one form or another since 1929, and owner Rick Paul says it's the oldest continuous restaurant in Frankfort, the state capital.

Rick hasn't spent much on signage for sure but don't let that deter you from the good food on the inside. Three small tables and 10 counter stools is pretty much it, except for some picnic tables on an outside patio, weather permitting.

"We like to keep our food simple and fresh," says Rick. We serve top notch ingredients and buy locally and fresh whenever we can."

A couple of large portable cooking smokers outside hints what is one of the big sellers. . . Memphis-style pulled pork bar-b-que. Rick also does ribs and smoked cornish game hens.

Rick's also promotes his "Cajun flair" by offering up dishes you don't just find anywhere. Crawfish pie, fried oyster po-boy, New Orleans muffaletta, crab cake sandwich, fried soft shell crab sandwich, and chicken and sausage jambalaya, served with buttered rye-bread.

There are a couple of side dishes worth noting. The grilled garlic potatoes with a touch of onions are superb as is the Cajun mix. Be careful with the Cajun

mix. When being served it comes with a verbal warning: "Be careful with it."

Rick has a couple of desserts that are about as good as it gets. His key lime pie is the real deal and his Kentucky bourbon pie is one of those where you'll probably want to buy a whole one to take home with you. How many times has something been advertised as "bourbon this" or "bourbon that" and you only have someone's word to the take as to whether bourbon really is used. Not so here.

Breakfast here features New Orleans-style beignets, French toast, pancakes, and, of course, omelets.

Rick Paul has an extensive history as a chef. Culinary school in New York, chef at Calumet Farms in Lexington and a past chef for the Lieutenant Governor of Kentucky.

Drive slowly; you don't want to miss it.

DINERS INFORMATION

Address:
114 Bridge Street
Hours:
Open, 8:00 a.m. – 5:00 p.m., Monday – Saturday
Phone:
502/330-4262
Price Range: $
Area Attractions:
State Capital

Sam's Restaurant

Good food and friendly service is what Sam's Restaurant is all about. It just very well may be the friendliest restaurant I've ever been in. Most certainly it's a top fiver.

Sam's, who evolved from Sam's Truck Stop on Highway 25, years ago, sits only a few feet from the Scott-Fayette county line, making it also close to the Kentucky Horse Park and Toyota Assembly Plant.

The waitresses, some of which have been there 20 to 30 years want you to call them by their first name. That's why they wear tee shirts with their names on them.

From the moment you open the front door you know the food will be good. A counter with six stools sits to the left facing the kitchen area, and nearby is a jukebox. Booths and tables allow the restaurant to seat close to 100 customers.

What a menu. It's jammed with breakfast, lunch and dinner selections. In all honesty there's almost too much to choose from.

Country ham, omelets, hot cakes, and oh that biscuit and real sausage gravy. And you've never seen such an order of grits and hash browns.

Lunch offers up an assortment of sandwiches, headed up by the Samburger. It's one of the favorites as is the club and fish. Spaghetti, meatloaf, catfish and chicken livers also rank real high as far as crowd pleasers go.

Sam's Restaurant offers up

prime rib night every Friday night. You may want to get there early.

There's not much their restaurant doesn't have from seafood to steaks to chops, and owners Cindy and Kevin Tipton strive to present quality, well proportioned Kentucky home cooked meals. They use original recipes whenever possible.

DINERS INFORMATION

Address:
1978 U.S. Highway 25, Lexington Road
Hours:
Open, 7:00 a.m. — 11:00 p.m. — Monday — Saturday
7:00 a.m. — 2:00 p.m. Sunday
Phone:
502/863-5872
Price Range: $
Area Attractions:
Toyota Plant

Science Hill Inn

SHELBYVILLE, KENTUCKY

Some folks say it's the best place in Kentucky to have lunch. Others say it's the best place for dinner. It has even been described as the best restaurant in all of Kentucky.

Whether any of the above is true or not is of little consequence, because Science Hill Inn is indeed one very good restaurant.

Terry and Donna Gill, along with daughter Ellen, have put together a warm, classy restaurant that is very sophisticated in a simple sort of way. It's definitely not a baseball cap and tee-shirt sort of place, but it's not uppity either.

Located in a historic structure in downtown Shelbyville that served as an all-girls school from 1825 until 1939 and known as Science Hill School, the Gills decided it was the perfect place to open a first class restaurant. And they did in 1978.

The country elegance is amplified by roomy tables and comfortable chairs and fits rather nicely with a menu that keeps it simple. No cutesy names to confuse diners into selecting something they didn't intend to order.

Donna and Ellen are bonified chefs and it shows with what they turn out.

Appetizers like grilled shrimp and country ham skewers are marinated in a mixture of mustard, Makers Mark bourbon and brown sugar, and served on a bed of wild rice and toasted pecans. That's one of several offered.

110

As you might expect, rib eyes, beef tenderloin, chicken (sautéed, grilled and fried), pork chops, and salmon are offered. But it's the Carolina shrimp with grits that jumps off the menu. The shrimp is sautéed with butter and onions. Creole seasoning is added and it is then served over a bed of cheese grits and topped with bacon.

As good as the dinners are at Science Hill Inn, lunch is just as good. Burgundy beef and noodles, hot browns, deviled crab, turkey, fried chicken and country ham are just a few of the offerings. And those desserts! Save room, especially for the brown sugar pie. It's brown sugar, eggs and cream baked in an almond crust topped with whipped cream.

DINERS INFORMATION

Address:
525 Washington Street
Hours:
Tuesday – Sunday, 11:30 a.m. – 2:30 p.m.
Evenings only on Friday and Saturday, 5:30 p.m. – 8:30 p.m.
Phone:
502/633-2825
Price Range: $$
Area Attractions:
Horses

The Stone Hearth

ELIZABETHTOWN, KENTUCKY

For years, since 1977, the Stone Hearth has been one fine restaurant. From the time you walk through the heavy wood doors, customers have the sense of a warm, relaxed, casual feeling, but at the same time an elegant, upscale atmosphere.

From the stone hearth fireplace to the gigantic salad bar, to the big overstuffed chairs to the cozy booths, this is an enjoyable place to eat.

When you first sit down, you are almost immediately presented with some fresh baked rolls and delicious strawberry butter. And it only gets better.

Alyce Skees and Martha Pride have consistently maintained quality over the years and they've built a reputation with their French Onion soup and incredible salad bar. Not only does this salad bar look good, it is good, and very well may be the best in all of Kentucky.

The Stone Hearth is noted as a great place to lunch, and even though they have an "express menu" where your order is prepared in less than 15 minutes, may I suggest that you relax and order from the full lunch menu.

A great selection of salads is offered and two of the more popular choices are the Strawberry Patch and the Honey Pecan Chicken Salad. Their names alone make you want one. An assortment of sandwiches, including one of my favorites, the Black and Blue Burger (anything with bleu cheese crumbles gets my vote) is offered.

The rib eye, grilled salmon and the hot brown are "can't go wrong" orders that make sure you don't leave hungry.

The evening meal offers an array of fish to include broiled cod, bourbon glazed grilled salmon, and broiled mahi mahi finished with a Malibu Rum sweet and sour sauce.

An assortment of steaks, chops, chicken and pasta dishes also highlight an extensive menu.

"The lounge and bar area are referred to as Martha's Vineyard," says Martha Pride. "And the rest of the place we refer to as Alyce's Restaurant. Bet you don't have two owners whose names work better than that."

DINERS INFORMATION

Address:
1001 N. Mulberry Street
Hours:
Open, Lunch 11:00 a.m. — 2:00 p.m., Monday — Friday
11:00 a.m. — 2:00 p.m., Sunday Buffet
Dinner, 5:00 p.m. — 9:00 p.m., Monday — Saturday
Phone:
270/765-4898
Price Range: $$
Area Attractions:
Coca-Cola Museum, Civil War History

Three Suns Bistro

NICHOLASVILLE, KENTUCKY

"I ate here three times in one day," said one customer.

That says a lot about this restaurant, especially when considering they don't serve breakfast. The customer went on to explain she ate lunch, dinner, and came back later for dessert.

Sherrie and husband Ben Pauley own and operate Three Suns. The locals know all about it, but visitors might easily drive past the converted fast food location.

"We actually need more space," says Sherry. "We fill up pretty quick."

Even if they do move to a larger location you can bet the food will continue to be outstanding. Sherry personally handles the kitchen area with the skills of a seasoned chef, while Ben takes care of the "out front" duties.

Reservations are recommended on the weekend, but don't expect anything fancy. There's no fancy bar to sit at while waiting for a table. But the available alcohol choices are top shelf with a complete wine list.

It's just about a guarantee that everything you order here will be good. It starts with crab cakes topped with a tomato caper relish made from scratch.

Then there's the sweet potato bisque and lobster

bisque. The appetizers are almost a meal. But in case you have room you've got to order the prime rib. Oh, did I mention the bread? Warm French bread served with soft butter ready to spread.

Three Suns Bistro is worth a visit for sure.

DINERS INFORMATION

Address:
Brannon Crossing, 298 East Brannon Rd. (off Nicholasville Rd.)
Hours:
Lunch, 11:00 a.m. – 3:00 p.m., Monday – Saturday
Dinner, 5:30 p.m. – 10:00 p.m., Monday – Saturday
11:30 a.m. – 3:00 p.m., Sunday
Phone:
859/881-8225
Price Range: $$
Area Attractions:
Camp Nelson Civil War Park

Wallace Station

The old building that is home to Wallace Station used to be a depot. Then it was a post office. After that an old country store. But today it is a fantastic deli/bakery in the middle of horse country on a Kentucky Scenic Byway.

The railroad tracks that once ran beside the building have been long gone, but thank goodness Jared and Paige Richardson decided a few years ago to open this unique eatery "out in the country."

The customers here come from the horse people, stable hands, riders, trainers and owners. If you listen carefully you just might hear a tip or two about a future Derby hopeful.

"We're all about fresh and doing it with Kentucky products," explains Jared. "I like simple food and let the food speak for itself."

Richardson is a graduate of the Culinary Institute of America in Hyde Park., NY, and has worked in Woodstock, NY and Hilton Head, SC.

Wallace Station specializes in sandwiches (hot and cold), fresh homemade soups and salads, and sides like creamy potato salad, vinegar slaw and creamy cole slaw.

Back to those sandwiches. They've got cute little names, but it all boils down to Cajun beef, reuben, hot ham and brie, ham and pi-

mento, turkey and muffaletta. There's one, however, that really catches your eye. It's the "inside out hot brown." It's a hot brown made into a sandwich! The turkey, ham, smoked bacon, tomato, white cheddar sauce are grilled on two hugh slices of homemade white bread. Delicious! Please note that all of these sandwiches are so big you may want to split an order.

Meatloaf, country ham, turkey and chicken salad are among the "cold" offerings.

The bakery side of Wallace Station is worth the trip. The giant homemade cookies, brownies and pastries are delicious. But it's the chocolate bourbon bon-bon that jumps out of the glass bakery case at you. Don't leave for home without at least one.

Wallace Station also does breakfast.

DINERS INFORMATION

Address:
3854 Old Frankfort Pike
Hours:
Open, 8:00 a.m. — 5:00 p.m., Monday — Saturday
11:00 a.m. — 4:00 p.m., Sunday
Summer hours vary
Phone:
859/846-5161
Price Range: $
Area Attractions:
Antiques, Horses

Westport General Store

Many small communities across America are often referred to as hamlets or villages, but in Kentucky they are sometimes called a wide-place-in-the road. Such is the case of Westport in Oldham County.

Westport General Store is the towns happening place. Will and Laura Crawford have taken the old store and turned it into more of a restaurant than a store. You can still buy a few things there, but it's their eatery that has been drawing all of the attention lately.

Actually the attention began when the Crawford's brought in a 323-pound wheel of Wisconsin cheddar cheese and sat it right in the middle of things.

Westport General Store, open for dinner, offers a staple of fresh made soups, salads, fried green tomatoes, bison burgers, hot browns, slow roasted chicken, tournedos of beef, fried bologna sandwiches and pulled pork platter.

And how about the red-eye shrimp! Its shrimp wrapped in country ham in a red-eye gravy reduction served on top of a creamy Weisenberger grits. You might want to make sure whatever you order you get an order of that bleu cheese cole slaw.

"We've actually gone more toward the restaurant side of things," says Laura Crawford." Once we got 100 seats, we were able to add a full service bar."

The bar also includes a very favorable wine list that only adds to the ambiance which, during the cold weather nights, includes

a wood burning stove in one corner of the dining room.

Westport General Store is only three blocks from the Ohio River and the restaurant even takes carry out orders to boaters.

"It's kind of neat. They call and we deliver their order in a golf cart right to their boat," Laura added.

The restaurant is only seven miles from LaGrange and seven miles from Goshen on Hwy. 524 just off of Kentucky Scenic By-Way Hwy. 42.

"We actually had a customer that drove in on a tractor, and another in a Rolls Royce at the same time," said Laura. "So it doesn't matter how you get here as long as you do."

There are a couple or three other unique shops in the immediate area, but not much more. This quaint little wide-spot-in-the-road is well worth a visit.

DINERS INFORMATION

Address:
1201 East Hwy. 524
Hours:
Tuesday – Thursday, 5:00 p.m. – 9:00 p.m.
Friday 5:00 p.m. – 10:00 p.m, and Saturday, 11:00 a.m. – 10:00 p.m.
Phone:
502/222-4626
Price Range: $
Area Attractions:
Antiques, Ohio River

Woodford Reserve Distillery

Who would have ever thought you could have lunch at one of Kentucky's top distilleries? But you can.

This meticulously restored historic distillery weaves a story that salutes the early day "bourbon pioneers" and their relationship to this particular location in Woodford County.

Sitting on the banks of Glenn's Creek, this 78 acre site takes advantage of the picturesque rolling hills of the countryside. A trip here allows visitors to see the old 1800's copper pot stills, and learn how America's only native spirit was crafted at this location almost 200 years ago.

The distillery offers a Picnic on the Porch for visitors from April through October. It's a casual affair served on the Visitor Center Terrace, overlooking the beautiful limestone architecture of this National Historic Landmark.

Chef-In-Residence, David Larson, was brought to Woodford Reserve in 1996 to serve up a cuisine that matched the perfection of their bourbon. And today, Larson coordinates and prepares all of the gourmet cuisine for special events at the distillery.

Chef Larson likes to focus on using Kentucky produce and food products in his culinary presentations, and over the years he has developed his own, unique version of contemporary southern cuisine. He has been an award winner for several of his uses of

120

Woodford Reserve in his culinary practice.

Picnic on the Porch is an a la carte menu that features a variety of seasonal sandwiches, salads and delicious desserts. It is served Tuesday through Saturday only from 11:30 a.m. to 2 p.m. No reservations are required.

A visit here is much more than a dining experience. It's a chance to see some of Kentucky's most beautiful scenery, legendary horse farms, and at the same time get an education about one of the states most famous products - - bourbon whiskey.

Address:
McCracken Pike
Hours:
Tours, 10:00 a.m., 11:00 a.m., 1:00 p.m., 2:00 p.m., 3:00 p.m.
Tuesday – Saturday
1:00 p.m., 2:00 p.m., 3:00 p.m., Sunday (April – October)
Closed major holidays
Phone:
859/879-1934
Price Range: $$
Area Attractions:
Horse Farms

Woody's at the Glyndon

Owner Andrew Jones has created two restaurants in one at his Woody's Restaurant in the old historic Glyndon Hotel in downtown Richmond on the corner of Third and Main Streets.

On the first floor is the casual, but nice, dining lounge with a full scale bar, and then there's the simple, but elegant main dining room on the mezzanine level of the hotel. You can order from the full menu in the lounge, but it's the dining room that sets Woody's at the Glyndon apart. It is upscale yet comfortable and casual. The 1940 era knotty pine panels blend nicely with the seven, nine-foot by six-foot windows and the fourteen foot high ceilings. The natural light and several gigantic mirrors give the room a much larger feeling than it really is.

Jones has come a long way from the Fry Daddy and two plastic tubs he used when he opened back in 1991.

"I've tried to create a classic formal elegance with Southern hospitality," Jones says.

He has done just that with those beautiful white tablecloths and napkins that supply a beautiful backdrop for daily fresh flowers that adorn each table in the dining room.

As nice as Woody's looks, the food is just as good. In the lounge area you can get a burger and a Bud or a filet and glass of Merlot.

For an appetizer you may want to try the Bleu Cheese Shrimp. It's wrapped in bacon and broiled with blue cheese crumbles. And you've got to have a cup of the tomato bisque. It's the single most popular item in the restaurant.

122

There are lots of salads to choose from. The one called Woody's Sig-nature is what you've got to order. After all when you put your name on it, it had better be good. It consist of romaine lettuce tossed in house vinaigrette, topped with freshly grated parmesan cheese, grilled peppers, mushrooms and onions.

For your entrée, how about the Filet Mignon with Bleu Cheese Gratin prepared with minced onions, bread crumbs and bleu cheese crumbles. And for dessert, the Phoenix Hotel Pecan Pie is recommended. Jones has secured the recipe from the old hotel in Lexington.

The Glyndon Hotel, that once upon a time, hosted the likes of Clark Gable and Tex Ritter, is considered the oldest continuous run business in Richmond dating back to 1892.

DINERS INFORMATION

Address:
Third and Main
Hours:
Monday – Friday, 11:00 a.m. – 2:00 p.m.
Dinner Hours, Monday – Friday, 5:00 p.m. – 10:30 p.m.
Phone:
859/623-5130
Price Range: $$
Area Attractions:
Arts & Crafts, Eastern Kentucky University

123

440 MAIN	BOWLING GREEN, KY
AMON'S SUGAR SHACK	SOMERSET, KY
BOLTON'S LANDING	GLASGOW, KY
BREAD OF LIFE CAFE	LIBERTY, KY
CAMBRIDGE MARKET & CAFE	BOWLING GREEN, KY
CIRCLE R RESTAURANT	COLUMBIA, KY
CREEKSIDE RESTAURANT	CAMPBELLSVILLE, KY
DOVIE'S RESTAURANT	TOMPKINSVILLE, KY
FARM BOY RESTAURANT	MORGANTOWN, KY
FARMER'S FEED MILL	LEITCHFIELD, KY
FEDERAL GROVE	AUBURN, KY
BRICKYARD CAFE	FRANKLIN, KY
GEORGE J. ELLIS DRUGS	GLASGOW, KY
HARPER'S CATFISH	SCOTTSVILLE, KY
HISTORIC LODGE RESTAURANT	RENFRO VALLEY, KY
JEAN'S RESTAURANT	MOUNT VERNON, KY
JUDY'S CASTLE	BOWLING GREEN, KY
KENTUCKY DEPOT	STANFORD, KY
LEE'S FORD MARINA RESTAURANT	SOMERSET, KY
LIGHTHOUSE RESTAURANT	SULPHUR WELL, KY
LUCY TUCKER'S ON MAIN	GREENSBURG, KY
THE PORCH RESTAURANT	RUSSELL SPRINGS, KY
PORKY PIG DINER	PIG, KY
ROY'S BAR-B-QUE	RUSSELLVILLE, KY
SAHARA STEAKHOUSE	CAVE CITY. KY
TELLIE'S CAFE	SCOTTSVILLE, KY

SOUTH CENTRAL
REGION

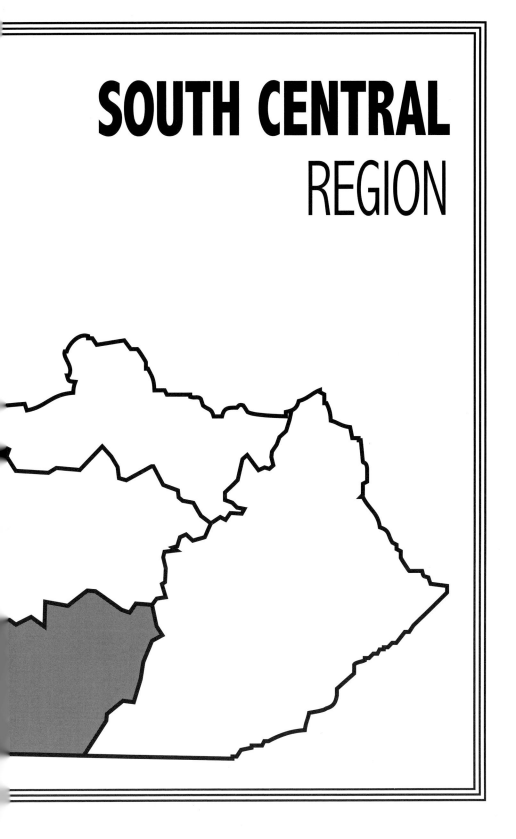

440 Main

4 40 Main has two front doors. Enter on the right side and you walk into a delightful bar area that offers an assortment of seating. From high back booths, to tables and chairs, to seating at an oversized bar, customers often don't have a choice, because it's so busy. Naturally food and drinks are served in this area.

Choose the door on the left and you will see a very elegant dining space in a shotgun style room, featuring a tin ceiling that gives patrons a clue that this is an old building.

The white table cloths, napkins, and just-right lighting lends itself to casual or special occasion dining.

Tom and Micki Holmes decided several years ago to make this downtown eatery, on historic Fountain Square, one that would reflect their native Cajun upbringing. Being from Monroe, LA., they wanted to give Bowling Green (a town with lots of good restaurants) an opportunity to experience real upscale Cajun fare. They've done it!

I must confess, one of my favorite things to eat is jambalaya. I have eaten it all over the country, including New Orleans and Lafayette, LA., and the jambalaya at 440 Main is the best.

Served in an oversized bowl, the shrimp, chicken breast chunks, Andouille sausage, sautéed peppers,

126

onions, celery and rice are blended into a spicy, spicy dining experience.

A caution to you: Ask the waiter what the heat factor is at the particular time you are there. Although the jambalaya is always good, the heat varies depending on who is cooking. This item is on the bar menu, but can be ordered on the restaurant side.

Other menu selections include a large list of items that are not necessarily Cajun or spicy. The cuisine would be considered American while many of the specials offer a Cajun flair.

Appetizers begin with pecan fried lamb chops, Roquefort and walnut stuffed dates, or how about Cajun spring rolls. Seafood selections include wild coho salmon with balsamic honey glaze, or pan-fried crab cakes with roasted corn and black bean salsa. Beef items are 8-ounce bayou fillet topped with fried oysters, or filets highlighted with bourbon spiked herb butter.

If you visit 440 on a weekend, you will probably catch some live entertainment on the bar side, and if the weather is good, table seating is offered sidewalk-style. By the way check out the artwork hanging on the walls. It's for sale.

DINERS INFORMATION

Address:
440 E. Main
Hours:
11:00 a.m. – 9:30 p.m., Monday-Thursday
11:00 a.m. – 10:30 p.m., Friday and 4:00 p.m.-10:30 p.m., Saturday
Closed Sunday
Phone:
270/793-0450 or 793-9862
Price Range: $$
Areas of Interest:
National Corvette Museum, Lost River Cave, Beech Bend Park & Raceway

Amon's Sugar Shack

SOMERSET, KENTUCKY

At stoplight #7 you'll probably see the Shell service station before you see Amon's Sugar Shack right next door. But that's okay as long as you find it because it's good. Really good!

The Somerset eatery has been written up in Southern Living Magazine not once, but twice over the last few years, and a stop here will let you know they are not resting on their laurels.

Amon Stephens and his wife Rosemary opened the bakery/restaurant in 1951, and have since turned over the daily operation to son Doug, although the two of them are a presence on most days. Another son, Terry, heads up the kitchen.

The Sugar Shack has built a reputation on its bakery goods with some 70 varieties to choose from.

May it be suggested you try the butter pecan cake donuts, or the coconut covered cake donuts, or the cinnamon pinwheel donuts or the yeast glazed donuts, or the . . . . . you get the picture. They're all great!

But Amon's Sugar Shack is much, much more than just donuts, cookies, breads, brownies, muffins, bagels and pies. How about the biscuit and gravy like "mama used to make," with chunks of sausage. For lunch the chili goes great, even in the summer. Pimento cheese, salads, ham and tuna salads are also popular items. And, on Wednesday's turkey and dressing with all the trimmings for $5.95 has become a standard.

The day at the Sugar Shack begins around 3:30 to 4 a.m. with doors opening at 5 a.m. Customers can use the handy drive-thru or sit down in the friendly dining area.

128

Eighty-four-year-old Amon is proud of the fact that he and his family have been able to carve out lots of success in a very competitive business by offering what his customers want; high quality food, friendly service and a great atmosphere.

If you're lucky you'll make your way to Somerset and try a couple of the 150 dozen doughnuts the Sugar Shack produces daily.

And how much coffee is brewed to go along with all of this good food?

"I don't know," say Rosemany. "I know we just keep making it."

Address:
523 S. Hwy. 27 (Stoplight #7)
Hours:
Open, 5:00 a.m. — 6:00 p.m., 7 days a week
Phone:
606/678-4392
Price Range: $
Area things of interest:
Lake Cumberland

Bolton's Landing

GLASGOW, KENTUCKY

First opened in 1982, Bolton's Landing has changed hands a few times over the years, but in the process has managed to continue to serve good food. Probably one of the reasons is that although the owners might change, much of the staff hasn't. In the restaurant business consistency is good.

Owners Danny Young and wife Linda have improved on what was already good. The emphasis here is on fresh.

Quiches, pastas, pork tenderloin, catfish, steaks, prime rib and chicken make up a good portion of the menu, but it's those "angel biscuits" that Bolton's is known for. Spread a touch of butter and a spoonful of honey and slowly savor the taste. The biscuit recipe is from one of the original owners, and they are just as good today as they were some 24 years ago.

I've always been a sucker for homemade potato chips and Bolton's does not disappoint. They're not overloaded with salt. They left that up to me.

If you visit Bolton's during the colder months you may want to get a table in the main seating area just beyond the entrance foyer. A large three-sided stone fireplace is sure to warm the body and soul as you enjoy your menu choice.

As an added bonus at Bolton's Landing, Linda Young owns and operates Sweetheart Bakery in Glasgow. And guess where all of those fresh desserts at

Bolton's come from? You guessed it! May I suggest the buttermilk pie or the chocolate cheese cake with raspberry sauce drizzled over the top?

"Landing" is defined as a place to rest and relax. I want to add that it is also a place to enjoy your favorite food.

Bolton's Landing sits just at the edge of town on 31-E, a few miles from Barren River State Resort Park.

DINERS INFORMATION

Address:
200 Calvary Dr. (Hwy. 31-E)
Hours:
Open, Lunch, Monday-Friday
Dinner, Monday-Saturday,
 Closed, Sunday
Phone:
270/651-8008
No alcohol
Price Range: $
Area Attractions:
Highland Games, and Barren River State Park

Bread of Life Cafe

LIBERTY, KENTUCKY

When you are traveling along on Highway 127, just outside of Liberty, the Bread of Life Café seems to just pop up out of nowhere. It's inviting and it makes you want to pull over and see what's up.

What's up is a full blown restaurant owned by Jerry and Sandy Tucker and operated as part of the Galilean Children's Home in Liberty.

The Tucker's recognize that people have to eat and people have to work. They took these two elements and turned them into a very good restaurant, in an area that possibly might be underserved when it comes to good eateries.

The Bread of Life Café offers you standard fare of soups, salads and sandwiches. The sandwiches range from burgers, Reuben's, steak, chicken and even Manhattan hot roast beef on homemade bread.

The entrees, usually served in the evening include New York Strip, Rib-Eye, Sirloin, Country Ham and Shrimp dinners.

To go along with the full service menu is a buffet counter that makes it easier for people to eat hearty and quickly.

The vegetables and fruits are home grown and the breads and desserts are homemade. In fact the Bread of Life Café has a "sweet shop" within the restaurant. It's difficult to see it and not order something. The pies and cakes, added to an old fashioned banana split, or an ice cold choco-

late milkshake make sure that customers leave full.

The restaurant seats 150 customers and on most Saturday nights they offer live bluegrass entertainment.

Indeed the Bread of Life Café is a good neighbor, and, indeed, it is a good place to eat.

DINERS INFORMATION

Address:
5369 Hwy. 127
Hours:
Open, 10:30 a.m. – 8:00 p.m., Monday – Wednesday
10:30 a.m. – 9:00 p.m., Thursday – Saturday
Closed Sunday
Phone:
606/787-6110
Price Range: $
Area Attractions:
Clementsville Motorsports

Cambridge Market & Cafe

BOWLING GREEN, KENTUCKY

Cambridge owner Mike Hughes will tell you up front, "We are a busy, busy restaurant."

This downtown area eatery is a very popular noon time venue and the customers don't seem to mind the occasional line that sometimes backs out the front door. It's one of those place-your-order-call-your-name-restaurants, so the line moves pretty quickly.

The Cambridge Square shopping center on Fairview Avenue is a crowded little strip center at noon. The advice is be patient, a parking slot will free up in no time. Any short wait you may have is well worth it.

"The reason for our success is that our customers know they are getting quality food," Hughes explains. "We take pride in preparing our menu items from scratch with fresh ingredients."

The quality and freshness comes in the form of daily homemade soups, fresh salads, vegetables and fruits. And, oh those sandwiches. The meats, cheeses and dressings make the Cambridge sandwiches selection almost unlimited. They also sell their items by the pound for carryout, and you ought to see that line.

Don't just think Cambridge Market and Café is limited to sandwiches. Hot browns, meat loaf and pork loin are a staple, and it is not unusual for them to offer up a daily special.

The regulars at Cambridge will tell you that as good as the main course is, it may be the desserts that set them apart, especially the cheesecake.

134

Their signature item?

"It's our chicken salad," says Hughes. "It's made with grapes and nuts, and everybody seems to love it."

The 100-seat restaurant is one of many good ones in Bowling Green, but I can tell you this is outstanding

They close during the first week of July, and they begin opening for evening meals after the first of the year, 2007.

DINERS INFORMATION

Address:
830 Fairview Avenue
Hours:
Open, 9:00 a.m. – 5:30 p.m., Monday through Friday (beginning January 2007, open until 8:00 p.m.
10:00 a.m. – 3:00 p.m., Saturday
Closed Sunday
Phone:
270/782-9366
Price Range: $
Area Attractions:
National Corvette Museum, and Beech Bend Park

Circle R Restaurant

The cover of the menu reads "A Kentucky Tradition Since 1947." You know if a restaurant has been in the same location under the same name and waitresses who call you Hon, sweetie and dear, then the food has got to be good.

And about those waitresses. Several have been at the Circle R Restaurant for over 30 years!

Owners, David and Ingrid Hawkins know the importance of keeping employees who understand the tradition of the Circle R and its relationship to the town of Columbia.

"Sandra Ford is our restaurant manager and she understands the importance of the Circle R and what it means to this community." David Hawkins points out.

It's easy to see that the friendliness at the Circle R is as much a part of the atmosphere as the knotty-pine paneling that hugs the walls.

"This restaurant has been here for so many years that the locals expect

it to stay open and serve good food," Hawkins added. "And that's what we aim to do."

The Circle R also has something else that for the most part has been lost in small town America. Curb service without a squawk box. A real person comes out and takes your order and also delivers it. Lots of people in this small Adair County town call ahead for carryout and have it delivered when they pull up.

Another thing that makes this restaurant unique is that it opens at 5:00 a.m. seven days a week. It takes three shifts to keep it going.

The food at the Circle R can best be described as comfort food.

"We're going to offer what our customers want," says Hawkins, "But I want to continue looking at what we can do to make this restaurant better, both with the food and facility."

The Circle R offers a grilled fish everyday, but it's the fried fish that is the most popular item.

The burgers are hand-patted with onions. The country fried steak is covered with real milk gravy and the fried chicken. . .well you've got to taste it to describe it. It's all about southern style cooking, you know, like Penn's country ham and red-eye gravy. Food like this is not available at most other places.

Seven days a week the Circle R has daily specials. They've also got your traditional steak, seafood and chicken dinners.

Get there early. And if you find some of the locals giving you the eye it's probably because you have their regular seat. That's okay, take your time. They'll gladly wait.

DINERS INFORMATION

Address:
712 Russell Road
Hours:
Open, 5:00 a.m. – 8:00 p.m., seven days a week
Phone:
270/384-3212
Price Range: $
Area Attractions:
Green River Lake

Creekside Restaurant

CAMPBELLSVILLE, KENTUCKY

The first thing you may wonder when you pull up in front of Creekside Restaurant is "where's the creek?" There used to be one at the restaurant's previous location, before fire destroyed the building. That restaurant had been in the downtown for almost six years.

Owner Terry Pennington decided it was time to move to a location he could expand and better serve his customers from Taylor County and all of the others that drive in from surrounding towns. The "new Creekside" seats 250.

"We've got a great reputation for our home-style buffet," Pennington says.

And is it ever good!

Chicken tenders, fish, fried corn bread, Penn's country ham, home-grown vegetables, chili, potato soup, and homemade desserts are just a small sampling of what you'll have to choose from. And if you get there on a Friday or Saturday night you may want to make sure the clothes you wear are expandable.

Friday night is all-you-can-eat catfish and Saturday night it's all-you-can-eat prime rib.

Now let it be known that Creekside Restaurant is much more than a buffet house. They have an extensive lunch and dinner menu featuring fish platters, shrimp baskets, roast beef, stir-fried chicken, stuffed tomatoes, sandwiches, Caesar salad, chicken salad, steaks, beef tips, frog legs, breaded oysters, chicken, country ham, pork loin and baby back ribs.

Creekside is far from a one dimensional restaurant.

Visitors to the area may want to check out nearby Emerald Isle Marina on Green River Lake, only a short drive from Creekside. They have some luxury condominium-style lodging rooms near the edge of the lake and they're available year round.

DINERS INFORMATION

Address:
1837 New Lebanon Road
Hours:
Open, 11:00 a.m. – 9:00 p.m., Sunday – Thursday
11:00 a.m. – 10:00 p.m., Friday and Saturday
Phone:
270/465-7777
Price Range: $
Area Attractions:
Green River Lake

Dovie's Restaurant

TOMPKINSVILLE, KENTUCKY

Dovie's is very difficult to describe. First of all you can't phone in an order, because they don't have a phone. You can't pick up a menu because they don't have one of those either. You don't have to worry about breaking a plate at Dovie's, because they don't have any of those.

But what they do have are delicious Dovie burgers, and in spite of everything that's been pointed out they've been in business since 1940 selling up to 1,100 burgers a day.

Manager Becky Webb who has worked here off and on since the mid-70s says on an average day they'll sell 600.

"We also sell lots of hot dogs, ham and egg sandwiches and fried bologna," she says. "But it's the burgers that most people come here for."

Several of the ladies at Dovie's have worked there for over 35 years and they have seen the world change around them. But not much has changed at Dovie's.

A simple metal-type building with a horseshoe shaped counter and 26 stools is pretty much it. In the middle of it all are two large vats that contain soy bean oil in which the large burgers are prepared.

Everything is served on wax paper and Becky Webb is quick to tell you that the burgers are patted out fresh every morning.

Customers can get the burger dressed and most of the locals like to get the Dovie "special dressing added."

"Several years ago when all of the chain hamburger places

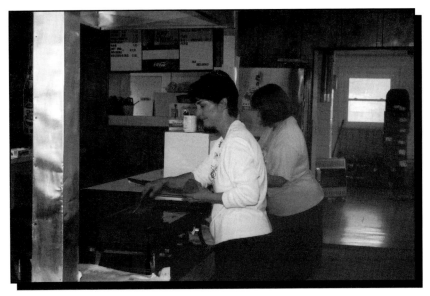

like McDonalds opened it hurt us bad at first," added Webb. "But pretty soon everybody was back."

Dovie's recently began offering homemade cake for dessert to go along with the commercially-cellophane packaged pies that are offered. Oh, by the way, don't leave there without a Dovie Burger T-shirt.

DINERS INFORMATION

Adress:
107 West 4th Street
Hours:
Monday – Friday, 8:30 a.m. – 4:00 p.m.
Saturday, 8:30 a.m. – 2:00 p.m.
No Phone!
Price Range: $
Area Attractions:
Old Mulkey Meeting House

Farm Boy Restaurant

MORGANTOWN, KENTUCKY

A trip to Evansville 36 years ago by Archie Phelps made him decide he wanted to open a restaurant in Morgantown sort of like he had seen in the Indiana town.

"He had seen the Farmers Daughter restaurant and came back and told his son he wanted to open a restaurant and call it Farm Boy," said Sharon Phelps, who along with husband AC, own and operate the Farm Boy Restaurant.

Today the restaurant operates two shifts, made up of lots of family members, from 5 a.m. til closing which can vary from day-to-day. They'll serve food as long as customers keep coming through the door.

"We start preparing the breakfast and lunches as early as 3 a.m.," offers Sharon Parker, one of several relatives who work at the Farm Boy. "People say our coffee is the best anywhere."

Breakfast is served any time, but that delicious fried chicken with their own special seasoning is served only on Sunday's.

Specials include chicken and dumplings, country fried steak and the best milk gravy you've ever put in your mouth, chicken livers, roast beef, baked ham, pork bar-b-que, green beans, real whipped potatoes, limas, cream corn, macaroni and cheese, fried apples, sweet potatoes and hash brown casserole, fried okra, fried squash and some unusual items like sweet corn nuggets, sweet potato stix and apple stix.

Up near the cash register is a big glass display case where customers can see up close all of those wonderful pies and cakes. The great thing about

its location is that because you probably won't have room for dessert, you still may want to get a slice to go. Good thinking!

Farm Boy Restaurant seats somewhere around 125 people and it's a common occurrence for it to be full and every customer can read the restaurants philosophy at the bottom of each menu. "We will never sacrifice food quality for lower prices."

DINERS INFORMATION

Address:
607 West G.L. Smith Street
Hours:
Open, 5:00 a.m. daily til customers stop coming through the door
Phone:
270/526-4649
Price Range: $
Area Attractions:
Green River Museum

Farmer's Feed Mill

LEITCHFIELD, KENTUCKY

Sometime when you least expect it a restaurant that serves very good food pops up. This is the case with Farmer's Feed Mill in Leitchfield.

It's one of those family owned and operated restaurants that explodes with a passion to turn out food good enough to make a special trip.

Farmer's Feed Mill is a three meal place – breakfast, lunch and dinner.

The family has a meat processing background, so you better believe they know their cuts of meat. And you better believe they hand cut everything on their menu.

Jill Blankenship is proud of the fact that her mom and dad, Winston and Jean Davis, are a big part of the restaurants success.

"Dad cuts all of the meats and makes our sausage," Jill says. "That way we know we are serving up nothing but the best. My son Kyle is very involved here, too."

For breakfast they serve up a Farmer's Workers Platter that includes two buttermilk biscuits covered with scratch gravy, sausage, hickory smoked bacon and boneless pork loin. Two eggs cooked to order, come with it. Bam!

For lunch and dinner the selections are almost endless. The baked sweet potato with cinnamon, brown sugar, butter and marshmallow is very popular. So is the potato soup, and cheesy potato.

But as good as all the side dishes are, it's those fantastic meat cuts that set Farmer's Feed Mill apart.

The steaks, any cut you want, are awesome. The prime rib, seasoned

and smoked, is a pure delight, as are the smoked bar-b-que ribs. However, it doesn't get much better than the Farmers Big Chop. It's a 1 ½" thick honey cured, smoked and then char grilled cut. It's a must!

The eatery also does Friday night tilapia, mahi-mahi and catfish.

Just in case there's room for dessert, they offer up a Coon Hunter's Cake. It's laced with pineapple and oh so good!

DINERS INFORMATION

Address:
110 Sequoia Drive
Hours:
Open, 6:00 a.m. – 8:00 p.m., Monday – Thursday
6:00 a.m. – 9:00 p.m., Friday
7:00 a.m. – 9:00 p.m., Saturday
Closed Sunday
Phone:
270/259-0259
Price Range: $
Area Attractions:
Rough River Lake

Federal Grove

AUBURN, KENTUCKY

The folks at Federal Grove like to say dining in their place gives customers a taste of the Kentucky south.

The home was built in 1871 on land once belonging to Jonathan Clark, the older brother of George Rogers Clark. In fact, Federal Grove was the name given to the property.

Federal Grove is a southern eatery that also is a bed and breakfast, and they specialize in true southern tradition.

A garden salad gets you started. It is made up of lettuce, New York style garlic pita chips, and almonds, topped with a tomato based dressing that is sooo good.

The menu varies on a daily basis, but visitors will always be able to select from southern fried chicken, roasted pork tenderloin, grandma's scrumptious meat loaf or beef tenderloin roast that you can cut with a fork. If you get there during the right season (usually summer), you will dine on sweet corn, cooked in a traditional black skillet, sliced tomatoes, country style green beans, and garden fresh cole slaw. And by all means don't confuse the incredible pickles with Aunt Bee's.

Dessert is really special. A strawberry cake or the chocolate fudge pie makes sure of that. Note, we said fudge!

Eating at Federal Grove has been described by some

customers as "going to a friend's house for dinner." A typical old south country breakfast consists of country ham, biscuits and red-eye gravy and everything else that goes with it.

Lanny and Terry Harlow personally make sure that every guest is treated like one. Service is as good as it gets.

The grounds and home at Federal Grove are also a great photo op so be sure and bring your camera.

Address:
475 East Main Street
Hours:
By reservation preferably
Phone:
270/542-6106 or federalgrove@logantele.com
Price Range: $$
Area Attractions:
Shaker Museum

147

Brickyard Cafe

How do two guys one from Croatia and the other from Bosnia get together in, of all places, Kentucky and open an Italian eatery in both Franklin and Bowling Green.

Robert Stupar and Jake Simic first met in Bowling Green in 1995 through a federal refugee program.

Jake had owned a restaurant in Bosnia. He played soccer at the professional level, and at the age of 35 life appeared to be good.

That all changed in 1992, when his country was torn apart by the elements of war. His brother-in-law was already in Bowling Green, so that connection played a part in his decision to come here.

At about the same time Jake's life was in transition, so was that of Robert's.

He was 22 and had just completed a tour of duty in his country's military, and worked as a baker. A war in Croatia led to his decision to leave.

Jake and Robert met on Jake's first day in Bowling Green. The rest is history.

They talked of their life before leaving their home land. And they talked about their futures that included maybe someday opening a restaurant. They saved their money and finally were set to go.

"We thought it would only take us two weeks to get open," Jake laughed.

Almost a year later they opened in Bowling Green.

And then the beautiful Brickyard Café in Franklin, just off of the town's public square

opened a few years ago. Only a stones throw from the historic court house the restaurant sits in an old brick building they restored. Built in 1912, it once was an old carriage house. An original elevator that, in its day, hoisted the carriages to the second and third floors for service. Today it is suspended on its original manually operated platform in the main dining room.

The Brickyard seats some 200 patrons in the dining area, and an adjoining full service bar allows others to sit at the 30-foot bar or several smaller tables in the room.

The menu is of Mediterranean influence with an Italian flair. Jake had lived 100 miles from the Italian border in Bosnia, while Robert was just 30 miles away in Croatia.

An assortment of crispy calamari, steamed mussels and lemon pepper shrimp are just a few of the appetizer selections. I must tell you that whatever salad choice you make choose one that you can top off with gorgonzola dressing. It is probably the best in the world.

The Brickyards evening specials are always "the best." The sesame crusted tuna is definitely a keeper, as are any of their scallop dishes.

Menu entrees include delicious chicken saltimbocca, veal picatta, and pork scallopine. Pasta selections from cannelloni to lasagna, to blackened chicken alfredo, which is served with a parmesan and basil-tomato cream sauce. Wow! Is it great!

Address:
205 W. Cedar Street
Hours:
Lunch, 11 a.m. – 4 p.m., Monday – Friday
Dinner, 5 p.m. – 9 p.m., Monday – Thursday;
5 p.m. – 10 p.m., Friday and Saturday
Phone:
270/586-9080
Price Range: $$
Area Attractions:
Kentucky Downs Race Course, Kenny Perry Golf Course

149

George J. Ellis Drugs

For more than a century George J. Ellis Drugs has been in continuous operation. Although there have been several owners along the way, as well as a slight change of direction for the purpose and existence of George J's, there has always remained a spot for the locals to gather and enjoy something to eat.

At one time this downtown hot spot was truly a "drug store", filling prescriptions, selling cosmetics, tobacco products (pipes, cigars and lighters), toys, health and beauty aids, and even appliances for the home. But as has happened in many towns across America, the smaller, locally owned stores like George J. Ellis' gave way to the chains.

However, one of the stores assets was a breakfast/lunch area. For a number of reasons the crowds kept coming, particularly at breakfast. And as everything else, it continued to thrive. As the retail part of the business was eliminated, the restaurant side was expanded, and today the locals still make George J's a part of their daily ritual.

Breakfast here is special, especially the country ham, eggs, hash browns and toast. The menu has an extensive list that includes eggs, bacon, sausage, baked ham, omelets, breakfast sandwiches (egg biscuit, sausage biscuit, country ham or tenderloin biscuit). There's one called a sausage burger with egg and cheese. Lots of places have donuts, but do they serve grilled donuts? George J does. They

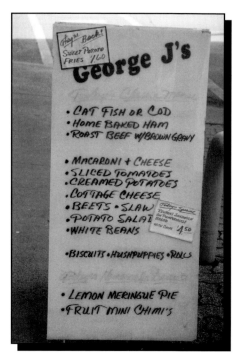

even have a biscuit and gravy that is served full or half order. That should tell you something about the size of it.

Another item listed is "conversation in liar's corner . . . no charge."

The lunch selections are a meat and two daily special. An assortment of delicious sandwiches is offered. Some of them are the chicken salad, BLT, homemade pimento cheese, burgers, chicken and a homemade soup of the day.

As you would expect at an "old" drug store, George J's has stayed true to form by serving up shakes, ice cream sodas, sundae and banana splits.

Something you don't find on just any menu is sweet potato fries and homemade potato chips. And how many restaurants in this book offer "keys made while you wait." Yep, over the years at this restaurant, you can always expect the unusual.

DINERS INFORMATION

Address:
144 E. Public Square
Hours:
Open, 7:00 a.m. – 4:00 p.m., Monday – Thursday
7:00 a.m. – 10:00 p.m., Friday and Saturday
Closed Sunday
Phone:
270/651-2161
Price Range: $
Area Attractions:
Barren River Lake

151

Harper's Catfish

SCOTTSVILLE, KENTUCKY

If catfish is part of a restaurant's name you can bet they serve it and it had better be good. At Harper's it is.

A two-tiered gravel parking lot greets you when you pull into the concrete block restaurant, and if you get there on a Friday or Saturday night there's a good chance you will see people standing out in the parking lot waiting to get in.

The 200 seat eatery that opened in 1978 serves up so much fried catfish, clams, and shrimp that it is mind boggling, and as good as they are, the homemade slaw may be the best you'll eat.

"We serve up over 150 gallons of the slaw," says owner Rusty Harper who has made Harper's Catfish a real working family business.

To prove the point, Rusty's mother who knows all of the locals was overheard introducing herself to a newcomer with, "Hello, I'm Rusty's mother."

Harper's is a three meal restaurant offering a typical breakfast and

lunch menu of eggs, country ham, pancakes, burgers, hot dogs, chuck wagon steak, and, of course, fish.

But it's at dinner when the crowd comes out. There are steaks, pork chops and chicken, but it's the fish, shrimp, clams, oysters, frog legs and hushpuppies that most people go there for.

A salad bar with that delicious slaw is quite popular. Oh, by the way forget the desserts. You won't have room. And also note Harper's doesn't take credit cards.

So much food is served with each order that almost everyone leaves with a "to-go box." There is a sign on the wall that reads "Please Do Not Ask For Extra Fish To Take Home With You." It's very appropriate at Harper's.

DINERS INFORMATION

Address:
3085 Old Gallatin Road
Hours:
Open, 7:00 a.m. — 9:00 p.m., Wednesday & Thursday
7:00 a.m. — 10:00 p.m., Friday & Saturday
7:00 a.m. — 8:00 p.m., Sunday
Closed Monday & Tuesday
Phone:
270/622-7557
Price Range: $
Area Attractions:
Barren River Lake

153

Historic Lodge Restaurant

RENFRO VALLEY, KENTUCKY

In some parts of Kentucky they call good food "country fixins." And that's what you get when you stop in at the Historic Lodge Restaurant at Renfro Valley near Mt. Vernon.

Renfro Valley, of course is well known over the years for its great show-stopping entertainment, so it's not often that good food and Renfro Valley are connected. But they are!

The Historic Lodge Restaurant is easy to spot on U.S. 25 not far from exit 62 on I-75. It's a log-like structure that over the years has been added to in order to meet the customer demand.

Breakfast, lunch and dinner are all part of the dining presentation here.

Fried country ham is a very popular item, as are those wonderful ham and cheese omelets. Naturally a place like this serves up biscuits and gravy, pancake stacks, buttermilk biscuits, fried apples and grits.

Lunchtime brings out the pork chops, chicken livers, homemade

meatloaf, pulled pork barbeque, and, oh yes, the country fried steak with gravy. There's plenty more with an assortment of sandwiches and salads, but you get the picture.

Dinnertime at the Lodge Restaurant is an event in itself. Sugar cured ham, pot roast, vegetable plate, chicken & dumplings, baked sweet potato, sweet baby carrots, pinto beans and that mouth-watering fried chicken done with a 50-year-old special recipe.

Renfro Valley has a footnote to their history and fried chicken. It seems that Valley owner John Lair turned down his friend Harland Sanders who wanted to launch his new secret fried chicken recipe that he was trying to get off the ground. Even though Lair didn't have that much excitement about the Colonels new business, they remained good friends.

As a footnote, how many restaurants do you know that list buttermilk on their drink offerings? They do here!

Address:
U.S. 25 at Exit 62 on I-75
Hours:
Open, 7:00 a.m. — 9:00 p.m.
Closed December 17 until 1st weekend in March
Phone:
800/765-7464
Price Range: $
Area Attractions:
Entertainment

Jean's Restaurant

MOUNT VERNON, KENTUCKY

I t's probably a safe bet to assume that you might not stop at Jean's Restaurant in Mount Vernon if you didn't know someone who had eaten there before, such as some of the locals. But on the other hand word-of-mouth spreads quickly in Kentucky, especially when it comes to good places to eat.

Located just off of I-75 at Exit 59, next to the Chevron Station, Jean's Restaurant is one of those eateries you don't judge from the outside. Don't pay any attention to the old rusted neon sign that sits atop the building, but instead check out the parking lot full of cars. The cars are empty because everyone is inside eating at one of the just over 60 seats.

Jean's is a country cooking place where you can get a hot, filling breakfast or a bowl of cereal. Pay close attention to the biscuits and gravy or pancakes or a choice of several omelets. They're all good!

The lunch specials change daily at Jeans and their regular menu items include things like chili dogs, Bob's Big Burger, B.L.T., country ham

sandwich, and, are you ready for this, pinto beans and onions over fried cornbread.

Jean's also offers steaks, center cut chops, pan fried chicken livers, roast beef and gravy and several seafood selections.

The desserts include pies, ice cream, hot fudge sundaes, coke floats and milk shakes.

By the way, Jean's offers a low-cal plate with a hamburger patty, peach, cottage cheese and sliced tomato. But by this time who's counting calories.

Bob and Velra Stewart have owned Jean's Restaurant for 11 years and one of their sayings is "nothing instant at Jean's but the service."

DINERS INFORMATION

Address:
1004 Brush Creek Road
Hours:
7:00 a.m. – 9:00 p.m. daily
Phone:
606/256-5319
Price Range: $
Area Attractions:
Renfro Valley

Judy's Castle

BOWLING GREEN, KENTUCKY

In a town chucked full of restaurants, Judy's Castle has managed to carve out a niche, and over the last 40 years has become somewhat of a landmark on Bowling Green's 31-W By-Pass. (It's no longer really a by-pass). The reason is simple. The restaurant serves very good home-cooked food.

Paul Durbin, owner/manager of Judy's Castle for the past 12 years, takes pride in offering the locals good food at a fair price. You don't leave here hungry.

Breakfast begins daily at 6 a.m. and Judy's is a popular place to catch up on all of the local and state politics. Traditional offerings that include omelets, grits, country ham, bacon, sausage, pancakes, biscuits and gravy are staples. One of the great things here is that Judy's Castle will go out of their way to prepare a special order fixed a certain way if that is your choice. It goes along with their slogan of "No hassle at the Castle."

It's lunch and dinner, however, that really standout at Judy's Castle. The restaurant can be described as a "meat-and-three" both on regular menu items or daily specials. A daily special may give customers a choice of turkey & dressing or pork chops. The vegetable selection could be mashed potatoes and gravy, turnip greens, green beans, white beans, black-eyed peas, baked beans, corn, apples and slaw.

The most popular from-the-menu selections are pork-bar-b-que, broasted chicken, spaghetti and pork tenderloin.

The big finish is the desserts. Judy's Castle has a reputation in Bowling Green for the best pies in town. Choco-

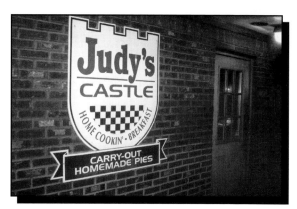

late, coconut, peanut butter-chocolate and pecan pies are made fresh daily. Don't be surprised if you see customers carrying out whole pies, two at a time, to take home. They are that good.

DINERS INFORMATION

Address:
1302 31-W By-Pass
Hours:
6:00 a.m. – 8:00 p.m., Monday – Friday
6:00 a.m. – 2:00 p.m., Saturday
Closed Sunday, closed major holiday weekends and week of July 4th
Phone:
270/842-8736
Price Range: $
Area Attractions:
Lost River Cave, Beech Bend Park, National Corvette Museum

Kentucky Depot

STANFORD, KENTUCKY

No matter where Gladys Reed opens a restaurant you can count on one thing for sure. The food will taste great.

Several years ago Gladys owned the Depot Restaurant in nearby McKinney, but then she decided to move over to Stanford, Kentucky's second oldest settlement, and just as everyone thought, the good taste of the food followed her.

Gladys will tell anyone within earshot that she likes to cook. There's an excitement in her voice when she tells you she has always liked to cook. With her and her staff, that includes several family members and loyal employees who have been with her for years, they are able to project a real passion for what they do.

At the Kentucky Depot Restaurant it's all about the food and keeping it simple. Nothing fancy mind you, just good food made from scratch with no shortcuts. And by the way, the restaurant is not a depot. It seems that the family had several railroaders in it and the original restaurant was located near the track in McKinney.

You can start with the open-flamed prepared rib-eye steak and the special seasoned pork tenderloin. When you put these with the delicious array of vegetables, you have one fine meal.

The real mashed potatoes, corn pudding, fried okra, green beans, pinto beans, baked apples, turnip greens and slaw are just some of the side dishes.

Other popular choices are the fried chicken, catfish, and maybe,

just maybe the best of all, center cuts of Penn's country ham. Put some of Gladys' incredible fried cornbread with any of these and it doesn't get much better than this.

Even if you're stuffed and don't have room for dessert you've got to order some anyway to take home. May I suggest the brown sugar pie? Gladys says people drive from miles around for a slice.

The Kentucky Depot Restaurant is a very busy place, and according to Gladys, they serve up over a thousand customers each week.

"Sundays are really big for us," she says. "We probably fix food for over 250 people."

Address:
119 Metker Trail
Hours:
Open, 10:30 a.m. – 9:00 p.m., Monday – Friday
11:00 a.m. – 9:00 p.m. Saturday
11:00 a.m. – 8:00 p.m. Sunday
Phone:
606/365-8040
Price Range: $
Area Attractions:
Cedar Creek Lake

The Harbor at Lee's Ford

When you combine outstanding food with a fantastic view it makes for a wonderful dining experience. And that's what you get at the Harbor Restaurant that overlooks Lee's Ford Marina on Lake Cumberland.

Located just seven miles from Somerset and four miles from the small community of Nancy, Lee's Ford is just off Highway 80.

The Harbor sits high atop of the lake and allows for patrons to look down, almost on top of many of the some 900 boats that are docked at the marina. The site of the dancing water, slow moving houseboats and friendly service adds up to an enjoyable meal, whether it's lunch or dinner.

Tiered outdoor decks allow diners to be closely connected to nature if they choose. However, the glass enclosed main dining room also presents a scenic view of the lake and boats below.

You don't have to be a seafood lover to appreciate the food here. Although Mama Lee's crab cakes, the Captain's Platter (oysters, shrimp, grouper, scallops, clam and hush puppies), or the grilled grouper are there for the choosing, the bourbon glazed pork chop, prime rib, rib eye and Mediterranean pasta are popular items, too.

An array of tasty appetizers that include grouper fingers, fresh calamari, southern fried banana peppers and shrimp cocktail are a great way to begin any meal.

The Harbor menu features a complete list of sandwiches and salads day or evening.

The restaurant has undergone an

expansion over the last couple of years by new owner J.D. Hamilton. Not only has he increased the seating capacity of the restaurant, he has also added an upscale bar area separate from the main dining area. An old antique bar highlights the area that also has several comfortable booths and tables where customers can also dine.

Lee's Ford is a destination, in that visitors can overnight in one of the several rustic cottages or rent a houseboat at the marina. When you go to the Harbor Restaurant, after your meal, take a walk down the 108 wooden steps to the marina Ship Store. There's some good shopping here. Oh, by the way, remember you have to walk back up those steps. If you ask nicely the restaurant staff will get you transportation down and back up the hill.

Address:
Lee's Ford Resort/Marina
Highway 80 (near Somerset)
Hours:
Monday – Thursday, 11:00 a.m. – 10:00 p.m.
Friday and Saturday, 11:00 a.m. – 11:00 p.m.
Sunday, 11:00 a.m. – 9:00 p.m.
Phone:
606/636-6426
Price Range: $$
Areas of Interest:
Lake Cumberland, Haney's Apple Farm

Lighthouse Restaurant

SULPHUR WELL, KENTUCKY

The location has been a restaurant for a long time, but it's been The Lighthouse Restaurant since 1987. Its one of those family style restaurants that the locals have been patronizing for years, but only recently, so to speak, has the "outside world" found out how really good it is. Occasionally a motor coach will be parked nearby and you might even see license plates from Indiana and Tennessee.

Tammy Deckard and her husband Rodney run the place and have done so since 1990. Mitchell and Norma Ervin, Tammy's parents operated things beginning in 1985.

The lighthouse replica that sits atop the building has no real significance other than Tammy's dad wanted it and had it ordered just before he died. It does make it a little easier to find.

The Lighthouse has your typical menu when it comes to fried shrimp, catfish, burgers and such, but what makes them special is their pinto beans and cornbread. However, the specialty of the house (what makes you want to go back again) is "your choice" of country ham, breaded catfish or crispy fried chicken. It's served family style with cole slaw, tomatoes, stewed potatoes, beans, fried apples, red-eye gravy and biscuits. You don't have to ask for the preserves or honey because it comes with it. At $12.95 a person it's a bargain. Oh, by the way, that country ham is Penn's, the Kentucky State Fair championship ham producer.

At many of the eateries in Kentucky, you need to save room for dessert. The Lighthouse is no exception. Butterscotch, cherry, pecan and peanut butter pies are difficult to say no to. So don't.

By the way if you happen to notice people waiting for a table even when there's others available, it's probably because someone is already sitting at their "regular one."

"Some people come in and want their usual table," offers Tammy Deckard. "They'll sometimes wait for over an hour to sit there."

Even if you think you might be sitting at someone's usual table, take your time. That's what they want you to do.

Sulphur Well (notice there is no "s") is six miles from Edmonton, the county seat of Metcalf on Highway 70, and while you're there you may want to walk across the road to the park and get a drink of the sulfur water from which the community was named.

Address:
Highway 70
Hours:
Open, Tuesday – Thursday, 11:00 a.m. – 8:00 p.m.
Friday and Saturday, 11:00 a.m. – 9:00 p.m.
Closed on Sunday and Monday
No Alcohol
Phone:
270/565-3095
Price Range: $
Area Attractions:
Barn Lot Theater

Lucy Tucker's on Main

GREENSBURG, KENTUCKY

Lucy Tucker's is a most unusual restaurant in that its menu changes every day. You see, they have three ladies who love to cook and they take turns in the kitchen. And whoever's doing the cooking on that particular day decides what she'll serve.

It works! And it's delicious!

Lucy Tucker is an old family name says Peggy Calhoun, who with husband Bill owns the restaurant.

"We rotate our menus out four times a year and leave it entirely up to who's cooking for the daily specials."

Lucy Tucker's looks like an old town house on the outside, and the uniqueness of the 1833 building on the inside is what really makes the atmosphere special. It only seats 26 at a time, so get there early. Visitors can appreciate some of the antique furnishings while waiting for the food to arrive.

Remember you'll have to let the server tell you the "special of the day," but some of the regular items are fried bologna dressed and served on toasted white bread. You didn't know bologna could taste so good.

Baked country ham on rye, smoked turkey with bacon and Benedictine, and roast beef with provolone cheese, purple onion, a hint of horseradish served on wheat are some of the sandwiches that make a trip to Lucy Tucker's worthwhile.

Eating in this restaurant's surrounding is an experience. It has the feel of being "down-home." The chairs and tables don't match, and customers are in two separate rooms, giving the feeling of being in an old southern boarding house. The recipes used here are those handed down from mother, grandmother, aunts and cousins.

At Lucy Tucker's on Main it's easy to see why they say they are simply southern.

Address:
105 North Main
Hours:
11:00 a.m. – 1:30 p.m., Tuesday – Saturday
Phone:
270/932-2658
Reservations accepted
Price Range: $
Area Attractions:
Historic Green County Courthouse

The Porch Restaurant

The front porch that expands all the way across the front of the restaurant is a dead give-away that you are at the right place.

The Porch takes pride in making many of their menu items from scratch, points out manager Connie Miller. "We really take pride in what we serve," she says.

This is an eatery that closes only on New Years Day. Several specials are offered throughout the week, with their homemade soups being among the most popular. Chicken noodle, potatoes, beef vegetable and chicken and rice are soups served at The Porch, and they don't come out of a can.

The restaurant also has a local reputation for their salads, especially the "large house" topped with chicken.

Friday night is catfish night and regardless of what time of the year it is people travel in to eat it. It's deep fried to a golden brown in a seasoned breading and served with your choice of two sides. One of the more popular sides is the mashed potatoes.

"We serve only real mashed potatoes," Miller says. "Always have, always will. When we run out there aren't any more until the next day."

Sunday lunch at The Porch is buffet style. In fact it's the only day they do a buffet.

The menu also offers rib eye steak, meatloaf, country fried chicken, grilled chicken, and

168

pork chops, and, of course, there's a large selection of sandwiches. Among them are burgers, BLT, clubs, fish, chicken, pork tenderloin and grilled cheese.

The desserts, all made right there in their kitchen, includes chocolate, coconut, Reese peanut butter and sugar free strawberry pies.

DINERS INFORMATION

Address:
234 Steve Drive
Hours:
Open, 10:30 a.m. – 8:00 p.m., Monday – Saturday
Sunday, 10:30 a.m. – 2:00 p.m.
Phone:
270/866-8988
Price Range: $
Area Attractions:
Lake Cumberland

Porky Pig Diner

PIG, KENTUCKY

You've got to be kidding!
Porky Pig Diner in Pig, Kentucky. No way.

On the surface you might think the name says it all, but it doesn't. Of course you can get the usual at Porky Pig Diner, plate lunches, prime rib, chicken strips, and even bar-b-que, and it's good. But their specialty and what the locals go for is the catfish. It's lightly breaded and cooked-to-order and served piping hot with all of the trimmings: hush puppies, potatoes and slaw.

Unless you are from the area, you are probably clueless when it comes to knowing where Pig is. It's a longtime Edmonson County community located on Highway 259 and Junction 422, a few miles off 31-W near Bowling Green. Customers might have to hunt a bit, but the effort is well worth the time. Something else well worth the trip is the peanut butter pie. Do not, and I repeat, do not leave without eating it there or getting a slice to go.

In case you want to prove you've eaten in Pig, Kentucky, owners Calvin and Ramona have a selection of T-shirts and caps for you to purchase.

If Sunday is your thing, Porky Pig Diner serves up a breakfast buffet.

The restaurant is small, comfortable, friendly and clean.

Address:
Highway 422
Hours:
Open, 6:00 a.m. — 8:00 p.m., Monday — Saturday
7:00 a.m. — 5:00 p.m., Sunday
Phone:
270/597-2422
No Alcohol
Price Range: $
Area Attractions:
Mammoth Cave, Diamond Caverns

Roy's Bar-B-Que

RUSSELLVILLE, KENTUCKY

Sometime when a restaurant opens it does so with a name that indicates their specialty of service. That same restaurant will evolve into serving other things just as good, but also still dishing out their original product.

Such is the case with Roy's Bar-B-Que.

It would be a safe bet that if you ask Logan County and Russellville residents in particular, 99.9% of them will know of Roy's.

The county is chucked full of history and famous happenings. Jesse James robbed a bank there, the Shakers were at South Union just a few miles down the road, and all those antique shops are at hand. And so is Roy's!

The mood at Roy's, from the time you walk in the door, is that you're like family. Visitors are often taken aback by the chatter from one table to another. It seems like everybody knows everybody at Roy's.

Roy's has been a family operation since its beginning in 1983. It started out serving from an old wooden framed camper, and has grown into a 100-seat restaurant that still sees customers lined up to get a seat.

What's good at Roy's? Everything.

Believe it or not, some locals will tell you they eat there almost everyday. Some say there are times when they eat there twice a day. That's why they can tell you what's good at Roy's.

Some days it's the bar-b-que. Some days it's the catfish. Other days it's

the fried chicken. But everyday it's those delicious homemade pies.

The Morgan family opened the restaurant and continue to make it even better. "Roy" is the name of one of Ralph and Jolene Morgan's sons, so now that they've put their name on the business, they will guarantee it to be good. So with a history that includes the father and mother, sons and daughters, and now the grandkids working their way up, the local newspaper, News-Democrat & Leader, went so far as to call Roy's a "Logan County landmark."

Address:
Hwy. 68 East and New By-Pass Road
Hours:
Daily, 9:00 a.m. – 8:00 p.m.
Phone:
270/726-8476
No Alcohol
Price Range: $
Area Attractions:
Bibb House Museum

Sahara Steakhouse

CAVE CITY, KENTUCKY

Since 1972 the Sahara Steakhouse has been turning out steaks, rib eyes, sirloins and filets. But the steak that they are best known for is their 20 ounce Sirloin for Two. All of their steaks are certified Angus beef and prepared on a charbroiled grill over an open flame. As good as the steaks are some credit has to go to the special seasonings that do indeed give them a full flavor.

Although steaks are the specialty, Sahara also serves up an assortment of chicken and seafood. The grilled chicken teriyaki, lemon pepper chicken, and orange roughy are some of the more popular offerings.

Owner, Brian Dale likes to point out that his Sirloin for Two is quite popular with those who experience the Wild Cave Tour at nearby Mammoth Cave National Park.

"When they crawl around on their hands and knees for six hours they exert a lot of energy and work up a hearty appetite," he says. "The Sirloin for Two solves their problem."

Most of us aren't going to do a Wild Cave Tour in order to enjoy the steak, so make sure you know you don't have to crawl on your hands and knees to eat here.

Over the years the restaurant has become known, also for its homemade vegetable beef soup.

"We've got customers traveling from Chicago to Florida who stop here just for a bowl of the soup," says Dale.

Salad bars are a dying breed at many restaurants across America, but several Ken-

tucky restaurants still provide them, and the salad bar at the Sahara is well worth talking about. Twenty-three different items are served and all of the dressings are homemade by Brian's wife, Emily.

The Sahara is one of those underrated restaurants that turn out very good food. It's a throwback to another era, and in this day and time when so many restaurants have a cookie cutter look, the Sahara Steakhouse stands out.

DINERS INFORMATION

Address:
413 East Happy Valley Road
Hours:
Open, 11:00 a.m. – 9:00 p.m. daily
Closed Thanksgiving and Christmas
Phone:
270/773-3450
Price Range: $$
Area Attractions:
Mammoth Cave/Caves

Tellie's Cafe

It would be a safe bet to assume that any outside visitors to Scottsville would probably not pick Tellie's Café to eat.

After all it is somewhat lost on one of the town's side streets. It's a clapboard siding house with a lot of "stuff" on the front porch, and the only thing that indicates it is a restaurant is a wooden sign in the front yard. But please, please find you a parking spot and go inside.

Tellie Stark opened her "neighborhood" restaurant some 20 years ago in a house that offers two rooms with several Formica-topped tables that will probably seat almost 40 when completely full. As you look around just remember, you're not there for the ambiance, you're there for the food.

Miss Tellie serves up the "best home cooking around."

"You won't find any better tasting food than this," offered one satisfied customer.

Tellie's is a lunch only stop. Fried chicken, pork chops, country ham or meat loaf will usually be the bill of fare. Also on the buffet hot table is corn, green beans, pinto beans, cornbread, slaw, and mashed potatoes. Sweet ice tea is a given with your meal, served in a real jar.

All of the locals know of Tellie's and her history of cooking great food in the area. From her days at Fosters and the Jacksonian Hotel (two former well known eateries), she has carried it over.

Remember, you're there for the food, not the scenery!

Address:
103 East Cherry Street
Hours:
Daily, 11:00 a.m. – 2:00 p.m. Closed Saturday
Open 12:00 p.m. – 2:00 p.m. Sunday
Phone:
270/239-4325
Price Eange: $
Area Attractions:
Barren River Lake

177

BEEHIVE TAVERN RESTAURANT AUGUSTA, KY
BIANCKE'S RESTAURANT CYNTHIANA. KY
CHAT-N-NIBBLE RESTAURANT EMINENCE, KY
THE COUNTRY GRILL DRY RIDGE, KY
DELITE'S DOWNTOWN MAYSVILLE, KY
GREYHOUND TAVERN FT. MITCHELL, KY
HUTCHISON'S GROCERY MAYSVILLE, KY
TWO RIVERS RESTAURANT CARROLLTON, KY

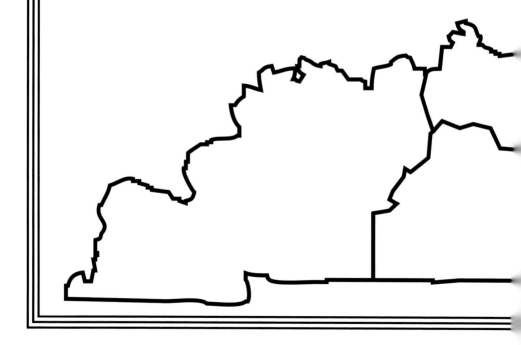

NORTHERN REGION

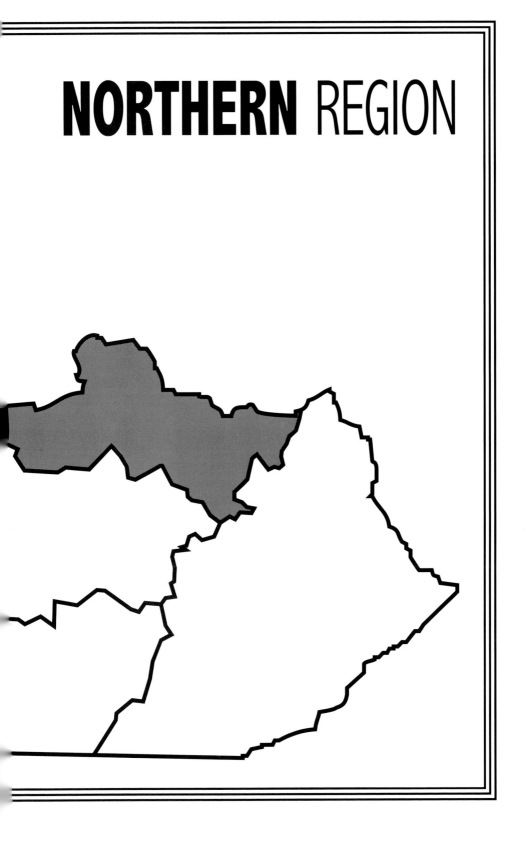

Beehive Tavern Restaurant

AUGUSTA, KENTUCKY

Luciano "Shawn" Moral owns and operates the Beehive Tavern and Restaurant in Augusta. For the last 20 years he has built his eatery into one of the outstanding restaurants anywhere around. In doing so he has put something back into the community by preserving a 1796 historic building.

It's almost hard to believe that a restaurant this good is in a town this small even if it is George Clooney's hometown.

From the time you arrive at the Beehive, even before you walk through the front door, you recognize that this is something special. Weather permitting and on weekends, a horse drawn carriage is there for tours of this picturesque village on the Ohio River.

You have your choice of dining on the balcony or in the main dining room where a piano player softly plays easy listening old standards and even takes requests.

The Beehive is upscale dining and even though there are no tablecloths on the tables, the linen napkins give it the classic accent to tie it all together with an abundance of candles and low light chandeliers. The distress, checkerboard stenciled wooden floor and the thick-silled windows give the Beehive a Shaker feel.

The menu is quite international in its presentation with dishes from Africa, Germany, Italy, and South America and, of course, Cuba.

The grouper and prime rib are excellent as is the braised brisket which is beef coated in brown sugar and cloves and slow

cooked for hours. It falls apart at the touch of a fork.

The Senegaleese chicken is a breast of chicken prepared with a tomato and peanut sauce along with crushed red peppers.

There is, of course, a lunch menu consisting of sandwiches, a catfish or country ham platter, pimento cheese, Rueben's on thick rye bread, and naturally there is the always present black bean soup. And as you would expect the desserts are all created in house.

But the real dessert of the evening, if you are there on a Friday or Saturday night, is when Chef Moral comes out and belts out a song or two with the accompaniment of the piano. Some of the locals say he is considered one of the great tenors of the world, having at one time understudied to the great Pavarotti.

The Beehive is a special place in a special town.

DINERS INFORMATION

Address:
101 W. Riverside Drive
Open:
Noon – 2:00 p.m., Wednesday through Saturday
Dinner 5:00 p.m. – 8:00 p.m., Wednesday – Thursday
Friday and Saturday, 5:00 p.m. – 9:00 p.m.
Sunday, 12:30 p.m. – 6:00 p.m. Closed, Monday and Tuesday
Phone:
606/756-2202
Price Range: $$
Area Attractions:
Antiques/Ohio River

Biancke's Restaurant

Judy and Tom Spicer operate one very busy restaurant. It has a classy country look to it and an extensive menu that would rival most of the so-called big city eateries. Biancke's has a clean, crisp look to it, with a dark green tile floor that looks like it has just been polished. The paneled walls are covered with pictures. Not pictures of famous people who have eaten there, but of customers who eat there. This is different, and only adds to the ambiance.

Biancke's does serve beer and wine as their choice of alcohol, and according to Tom Spicer his restaurant is the oldest continuous restaurant in the state.

Friday and Saturday nights look like grand central station. The place is packed and waitresses move from tables to kitchen and kitchen to tables almost on a run.

Baked spaghetti, hot browns, pork tenderloin, beer battered steak fries, and those fried green tomatoes with dipping sauce composed of

horseradish and tomato is a must order.

With several of the sandwiches and some of the entrees you can get a half or full order, and a small or big order on other items.

"We rely on the word of mouth to promote us," says Tom "We don't worry about the competition; we just do the best we can and rely on that."

Biancke's serves breakfast, lunch and dinner and Judy Spicer likes to point out that she doesn't have an instant package of anything in the restaurant.

"We don't cut corners," she says. "All of our salads are hand cut, dressings homemade, and coffee and tea fresh brewed."

DINERS INFORMATION

Address:
102 South Main
Hours:
Open, 7:00 a.m. – 9:00 p.m., Monday through Saturday
Phone:
859/234-3443
Price Range: $
Area Attractions:
Cynthiana County Museum

Chat-n-Nibble Restaurant

Sometime back in 1946 in Eminence a restaurant ran a local contest to name it. Chat-n-Nibble was the chosen name. The winner received a free meal and since then this downtown restaurant, for years, has played a role large and small, in the history of the town.

You've heard it said "if walls could talk." Well, these walls at Chat-n-Nibble have heard it all. The restaurant has been the social and political hub of the town and Henry County for years. Locals celebrated the good times and discussed the bad over a good meal. Early on it was a gathering place for local high school teams and fans after a big win or a tough loss. Chat-n-Nibble touched many lives. Always has, always will.

For the last 17 years Chat-n-Nibble has been owned and operated by Tom and Alice Fergerson, while Shannon Rucker oversees much of the kitchen duties.

Breakfast is a happening. Served from 6 a.m. til 11 a.m. Monday thru Saturday you can get anything from eggs to omelets, to steak and eggs, to eggs and tenderloin, and even fried bologna and eggs. Of course, pancakes and French toast are also available.

The lunch and dinner offerings include rib eyes, country fried steak, shrimp and white fish, catfish, burgers, roast beef, tuna melt, salads and desserts.

As in many small towns across Kentucky, downtown restaurants are located in buildings that were once used for something else. That's also the case

for Chat-n-Nibble. Before becoming a restaurant it was first a feed store, then a general store and later a "duck pen" bowling alley.

The folks in Eminence have never regretted it finally becoming a restaurant.

"One of the things we like to hear," says Alice Fergerson, "Is when people come back to town after being gone for 30 years and tells us our roast beef with mashed potatoes and gravy taste just like it did the last time they were here."

Daily specials at Chat-n-Nibble and those wonderful homemade pies (you've got to try the coconut cream pie) keep all of the locals still coming in after all these years.

DINERS INFORMATION

Address:
28 South Penn Street
Hours:
Open, 6:00 a.m. – 5:00 p.m., Monday through Thursday
6:00 a.m. – 8:00 p.m. Friday
6:00 a.m. – 5:00 p.m. Saturday and 11:00 a.m. – 2:00 p.m. Sunday
Phone:
502/845-9109
Price Range: $
Area Attractions:
Smith Berry Winery

The Country Grill

DRY RIDGE, KENTUCKY

Don't be turned off that the Country Grill is located near an interstate exit, near some of the well-known chains. Be thankful that a restaurant this good is convenient.

At The Country Grill they have chefs, not cooks. That's what regular customers will tell you, and Executive Chef/Owner Ed Smain genuinely enjoys feeding people and making customers happy with his food. Don't pay attention to the country craft décor when you walk in the door, but do pay attention to the outstanding food.

Smain, who along with his sister Laura, and brother-in-law Greg Melcher operate the restaurant, take pride in that their offerings are prepared from scratch.

For openers consider the stuffed mushrooms. They are caps stuffed with herb cream cheese and bacon, sautéed and served with garlic butter. And then there are those jumbo onion rings, hand breaded, of course. One order will serve two people. The salad dressings, ranch, blue cheese, thousand island, and olive oil & wine vinegar are all made from scratch, as are all their soups and various sauces.

"We make our own croutons and sell them by the bag full," offered Laura Melcher. "Customers also like the take home containers of our dressings."

They peel their own potatoes at the Country Grill so you can know the mashed potatoes are indeed real.

Just about anything on the menu is guaranteed to be good. The pot roast with carrots, mashed potatoes and gravy is exceptional, as is the primavera with char-grilled chicken, and Kentucky hot brown.

Friday nights at The Country Grill will always include a fish special, cod, catfish or trout. Saturday nights is prime rib, steaks or chops.

And now for dessert! All of them are homemade, which among them is a special one, a peanut butter cream pie. Wow!

Address:
21 Taft Highway, I-75, exit 159
Hours:
Open, 8:00 a.m. — 9:00 p.m., Sunday — Monday
8:00 a.m. — 10:00 p.m., Friday & Saturday
Phone:
859/824-6000
Price Range: $
Area Attractions:
Barkers Blackberry Hill Winery

Delite's Downtown

MAYSVILLE, KENTUCKY

For over 25 years John and Erato Kambelos have been nice to people. They've also turned out some pretty good food at Delite's in downtown Maysville!

Today Delite's is a local tradition. Anyone who has lived there even for a short period of time has probably eaten there.

It's nothing fancy, wooden booths and a few pictures on the wall depicting their home country of Greece. One in particular is the Acropolis in Athens.

Erato works the grill and John, for the most part, takes the orders. "He's the boss," she says. But somehow you don't quite believe her.

Delite's is clean and the grill is near the front window where passerby's can see inside and food cooking on the grill. There's lots of stainless steel and it sparkles.

Ten counter stools allow customers to be close to the action, and when you go there you'll hear a continuous banter between Erato, John and customers. It's all good!

The eatery is a gathering place for many of the locals, even on Saturday mornings.

Breakfast and lunch are the two meals served six days a week from 8 a.m. til 5 p.m. So you can catch one early dinner at Delite's.

The breakfast menu has its usual morning choices of eggs, ham, bacon and toast. But it's those sausage patties that catch your eye. No

cookie-cutter used here. They are hand-patted with the end result a piece of sausage about the size of the palm of your hand.

As you might expect they've got what is called a Gyro Classic. It's served with a creamy cucumber sauce on fluffy pita bread, but John will tell you quickly that their hamburger was voted "the best in town."

The politeness of John when he delivers an order to a table is noticed. "This is for you," he says as he gently places the order in front of you. He will also precisely arrange the dinnerware, the cup or saucer every time he comes to your table.

Another thing noticed at Delite's is often they don't write down the order until you get ready to pay.

Delite's Downtown is truly a delight.

DINERS INFORMATION

Address:
222 Market Street
Phone:
606/564-7047
Hours:
Open, 8:00 a.m. — 5:00 p.m., Monday through Saturday
Price Range: $
Area Attractions:
Old Washington Historic District

189

Greyhound Tavern

FT. MITCHELL, KENTUCKY

The Greyhound Tavern is a special place. It's a must if you're in the Northern Kentucky area. If you're not, you need to go there.

Originally opened in 1921 as an ice cream parlor, the restaurant has come a long way baby from a two-room building that sat at the end of the line where streetcars completed their journey south, made the turn around, heading back to Cincinnati. Today it seats some 200 customers and on a Friday or Saturday night you can expect a wait. But that's okay. The atmosphere is great and the "Tavern Room," offers a nice place to land while waiting for your table.

Any wait is worth it.

Butch and Mary Ann Wainscott, along with sons Gabe, Danny and Brad have established an eatery that serves up very good, mostly traditional, American food.

Of course their specials vary and keep their evening choices very interesting.

When you check out the appetizers, someone in your group has got to order the onion rings, if for no other reason than to look at them. If there are four of you, you'll only need to order the half order. There are four in the half and eight in the full order. One ring fills up a small plate. They are hand-cut sweet onions deep fried and served in a stack.

Steaks, chops, salmon, halibut, fried chicken and the evening specials that include filet stroganoff or chicken co qua vin.

An assortment of sandwiches, soups, salads and hot browns insure that there is something that will please

every customer who walks in. One item in particular stands out as something you don't see on everyone's menu is the hot slaw. It's thinly sliced cabbage with a sweet and sour dressing topped with jowl bacon.

The fresh flowers on each table only add to a great dining experience, and since there is no longer an ice cream parlor here, ask for directions to the nearby Graeter's Ice Cream shop.

DINERS INFORMATION

Address:
2500 Dixie Highway, I-75, exit 188
Hours:
Monday — Thursday, 11:00 a.m. — 10:00 p.m.
Friday and Saturday, 11:00 a.m. — 11:30 p.m.
Sunday 10:00 a.m. — 9:00 p.m.
Phone:
859/331-3767
Price Range: $$
Area Attractions:
Newport Aquarium

Hutchison's Grocery

MAYSVILLE, KENTUCKY

Hutchison's Grocery has been in continuous operation for over 155 years. It must be doing something right.

For Cissy Lester, the store's owner, it's pretty much a one person operation. There are times when she is so busy some of her good friends do, indeed, step up and help her out.

Hutchison's is one of those "grab and go" places. There are no tables to sit at, but there are a couple of benches. One is really special, it's a 1970s extra wide van seat. It just sits right there in the middle of the crowded aisles offering a place to rest while Cissy completes your order.

Country ham sandwiches are the specialty of the house as she serves up some 1,200 hams a year. She ships many of them to customers all over the country.

Hutchison's is without question one of the most unusual places to eat in all of Kentucky. The original wooden, glassless doors are there to greet you. Don't let the outside of the building fool you. Go ahead, go on in. When you do, you step back into another era. An old meat block rests to the right of the front door. It's not going to be moved anytime soon. It's a catch-all for candy items for sale.

Customers are patient. Cissy does it all and they know she'll get their order as soon as she can. She's fixing fried bologna sandwiches, city ham, pickle loaf and according to her, the best burgers in town.

Cissy actually started working at Hutchison's Grocery when she was 13 and has worked there off and on for 39 years.

"It's a 24/7 for me," she says. "But I enjoy it."

Being true to its name as a grocery store, customers still come in and get soft drinks, paper goods, milk, bread, can goods, and candy.

As busy as Cissy Lester is, she and some of her friends and neighbors find the time every October to put up a giant Christmas Village display in the right rear of the store for children and customers to enjoy.

"It takes six people eight hours to put it together and we keep it up til March," she says with pride.

Yes, when ole Micajah Hutchison put his name above the door back in 1850 he surely had no idea it would still be hanging there some 155 years later.

Address:
1201 E. Second Street
Hours:
Open, 9:00 a.m. – 5:30 p.m., Monday through Friday
 9:00 a.m. – 4:00 p.m., Saturday
Phone:
606/564-3797
Price Range: $
Area Attractions:
Old Washington Historic District

Two Rivers Restaurant

CARROLLTON, KENTUCKY

Kentucky has long been known to have one of the finest state park systems in the nation. Included in this is General Butler State Resort Park in Carrollton. Although traditionally now known for its food, General Butler has a non-traditional state park restaurant. Two Rivers Restaurant offers a full-service menu with something for everyone, including breakfast, lunch and dinner. The buffet is only served at lunch.

The name Two Rivers was derived from its location, sitting between the Kentucky and Ohio Rivers. The Kentucky River was once used to transport the state's exports to the Ohio River shipping docks where the products, including bourbon and tobacco, were then transported through the country.

The interior of Two Rivers is laced with old photos of the area which include nearby Carrollton.

Upon opening the menu, you will quickly notice that "bourbon" is a key ingredient in the preparation of many of the dishes. Bourbon pecan shrimp served with a delicious bourbon pecan sauce. Grilled Salmon, marinated in a special bourbon sauce.

Bourbon gives the food a Kentucky flavor, and besides that, it's good.

Two Rivers prides itself in its Happy Hollow Farm Chop that comes from Springfield, Kentucky. If you don't order this yourself, make sure someone in your group does so you can have a bite. The bourbon apples served with the chop is almost a meal in itself.

The catfish, trout, crab cakes, rib-eye, hot brown and country ham all appear on the menu. And so

does the lemon basil chicken asiago, a combination of angel hair, fresh asiago from Kenny's cheeses in Barren County and grilled chicken.

You probably won't save room for it, but just in case you do, the blackberry cobbler served in a hot, hot, hot cast iron skillet with a scoop of vanilla ice cream is a great way to finish your visit to Two Rivers. No alcohol served except in the recipes.

DINERS INFORMATION

Address:
General Butler State Park
Hours:
Open, 7:00 a.m. – 9:00 p.m. daily
Closed one week for Christmas
Phone:
502/732-4384
Price Range: $$
Area Attractions:
State Park

CEDAR VILLAGE	IRVINE, KY
ATHENAEUM RESTAURANT	WILLIAMSBURG, KY
AVENUE CAFE	MIDDLESBORO, KY
BILLY RAY'S RESTAURANT	PRESTONSBURG, KY
CHIRICO RISTORANTE	PIKEVILLE, KY
COURTHOUSE CAFÉ	WHITESBURG, KY
FRANCES' DINER	HAZARD, KY
HARLAND SANDERS CAFE	CORBIN, KY
KATHY'S COUNTRY KITCHEN	CLAY CITY, KY
MISS IDA'S TEA ROOM	INEZ, KY
MONA'S RESTAURANT	PIKEVILLE, KY
OPAL'S	MCKEE, KY
TEAPOT CAFE	HINDMAN, KY
WEAVERS HOT DOGS	LONDON, KY
WILMA'S	PAINTSVILLE, KY

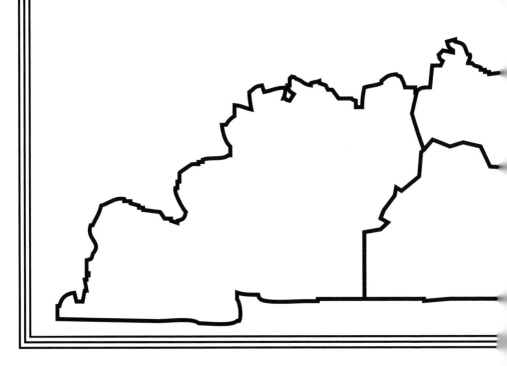

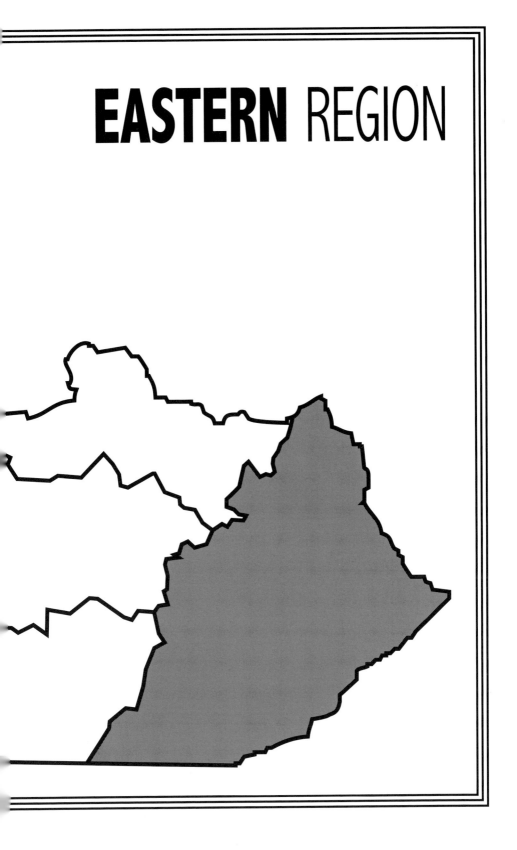

EASTERN REGION

Cedar Village

What a pleasant surprise when my wife and I pulled over at the Cedar Village Restaurant in Irvine, Kentucky for lunch. Lots of cars in the parking lot told us it was probably good. We were not disappointed.

Owner, Princess Benton, also operates the restaurant along with her son, daughter-in-law and grandson. And in Princesses words, "I get a little help from my husband, Ray."

A full menu offers up an assortment of home cooking at its best, but it is the buffet that quickly draws your attention.

"It's the real deal," said one customer in line. "The milk gravy and the mashed potatoes are the real deal."

Meat loaf, fried chicken, green beans, potatoes, corn, you name it and its there.

Princess is quick to tell you that she gets raves about her salad bar.

"It's all fresh," she says.

And then there are the desserts, with a soft-serve ice cream machine right next to them. I've got to tell you that when I thought I could eat no more, I spotted the peanut butter pie. Oh well, what's wrong with a small piece and a little dab of ice cream on top. I'll tell you what's wrong, nothing!

A full menu of salads, sandwiches, steaks, hot browns, meat and two specials, and burgers for those who want to narrow their selection down a bit. There's even a breakfast section.

198

Princess is from a family of 11 children, of which she was in the middle, and she has been cooking since she was 13.

"I'm from Buck Creek which is 11 miles from the Irvine Bridge," she laughs. "I've been cooking good food all my life."

Cedar Village seats well over 200 customers in a combination of booths and tables. This includes a couple of meeting rooms, which they open up on Sunday's.

On Friday and Saturday night and for lunch on Sunday, turkey and dressing, and baked country ham are featured, along with the mashed potatoes and milk gravy.

Oh, did I tell you about the strawberry shortcake? Well, you'll have to find out about that yourself.

Without question, Princess Benton serves up food fit for a king.

DINERS INFORMATION

Address:
1100 Richmond Road
Hours:
Monday – Thursday, 10 a.m. – 8 p.m.
Friday, 10 a.m. – 8:30 p.m.
Saturday, 11 a.m. – 8:30 p.m.; Sunday, 11 a.m. – 8 p.m.
Phone:
606/723-7777
Price Range: $
Area things of interest:
Cats Paws Antiques, Historic Downtown Irvine, Berea, Tator Knob Pottery

Athenaeum Restaurant

The Athenaeum Restaurant in the Cumberland Inn is unusual because it is actually a part of Cumberland College that sits just a short distance from the Kentucky-Tennessee line.

It is an old Williamsburg styled structure that houses a 50 room hotel, conference center, indoor pool, museum/gift shop and a very good restaurant.

The restaurant offers a menu that includes fried green tomatoes, grilled chicken Caesar salad, cornbread crusted trout that is rolled in a cornmeal crust and pan fried, a choice of grilled or fried pork chops, grilled salmon, liver and onions and hot brown.

The locals, however, will tell you that it's the buffets that really set the Atheneum apart from the others.

Sunday mornings only is a breakfast buffet offering fresh fruit, breads,

pastries, cereals, scrambled eggs, home fries, bacon, sausage, biscuits and gravy, grits and oatmeal, and, of course juices and other beverages.

Friday night features a seafood buffet with a vast selection of broiled and fried seafood. Crab legs and boiled shrimp accompanied by steaming hot vegetables, soups, and salads only add to the feast. An assortment of desserts makes sure no one leaves hungry.

It's home style southern cooking at the Saturday night country buffet. Pork chops, bar-b-que ribs, fried chicken, meatloaf, steamed vegetables, soup and salad are among the selections. There's even a chicken and dumplings offering to really make visitors feel "down home."

Themed lunch buffets are also served daily.

The Cumberland Inn complex is operated by the local college and staffed mainly by students working to earn their education while at the same time receiving valuable training in actual business management.

DINERS INFORMATION

Address:
649 South 10ᵗʰ Street
Hours:
Breakfast, 7:00 a.m. – 11:00 a.m., daily
Lunch, 11:00 a.m. – 4:00 p.m., daily
Dinner, 4:00 p.m. – 9:00 p.m., daily
Phone:
1/800-315-0286 or 606/539-4105
Price Range: $
Things of Interest:
Cumberland Fall State Park

The name of this café doesn't exactly describe in full detail what this restaurant is all about. Of course it's about good comfort food, but there's much, much more.

It's located in a turn-of-the century building downtown that once housed a funeral parlor. Following that, a produce market operated out of the building for the next 80 some years.

Judy Barton and husband Tommy have done a nice job in making Avenue Café more than just a place to eat good food. Many customers come in just to shop. Antiques, crafts, novelty gifts and collectibles are a staple in the café. They're scattered around the place so there are times that it takes on the feel of a treasure hunt.

Homemade soups and deli sandwiches are very popular among the locals, as is the freshly-made chicken salad.

"It's not unusual for us to sell a hundred pounds of it a week," says

Judy Barton. "We sell a lot of it to travelers between Florida and Michigan who have eaten it before."

Daily specials at the Avenue Cafe include hot roast beef & gravy, lemon pepper chicken, chicken and dumplings, meatloaf, stuffed green peppers, bar-b-que and baked beans, chicken casserole, beef stroganoff, pinto beans with wieners, kraut and a side of delicious cornbread.

"Most of our products are purchased daily so it will be as fresh as possible," Judy offers.

She likes to put her Italian heritage to good use with her "spaghetti day" every Thursday.

"It's my mother's recipe and no matter how much we make we sell out," she adds.

DINERS INFORMATION

Address:
1915 Cumberland Avenue
Hours:
9:00 a.m. – 3:00 p.m., Monday – Friday
Phone:
606/248-3958
Price Range: $
Area Attractions:
Cumberland Gap

Billy Ray's Restaurant

PRESTONSBURG, KENTUCKY

Billy Ray's in downtown Prestonsburg is one of those restaurants that you instinctively know was probably another business before it became a restaurant. Well sort of. In the beginning it was a bowling alley and then a pool room. It served food, but not the type of food it turns out today.

Now a days Billy Ray's is one busy restaurant, not only from the locals but visitors as well. Good news travels fast.

The restaurant has a warm, cozy feel but yet classy at the same time. Its long counter with some 20 stools today still serves customers at lunch but also serves as a place to display all of those cakes and pies covered in big glass dishes. Long ago tables and booths have replaced the pool tables and owners Sheila and Lee Collins, along with son Brian, are literally all over the place paying attention to detail and making sure the customer is happy.

At breakfast and lunch Billy Ray's is fast action all the way, with locals moving from table to table to shake hands and greet friends they know from surrounding towns. Much of the talk often centers on politics.

One local said, "You can be away from Prestonsburg for a month and 30 minutes at Billy Ray's has you caught up with everything."

But keep this in mind. If the food is not good they wouldn't talk politics there.

The food is very good!

Breakfast at Billy Ray's is a given. And at lunch their "poolroom hamburger" jumps off the grill, and if the double bacon cheeseburger deluxe is your choice please make sure you can open your mouth wide enough.

204

At night the lights are tastefully dimmed and candles are lit and Billy Ray's changes faces. Just a little.

On Friday and Saturday night it's surf and turf, prime rib, grilled shrimp stir fry, meatloaf, seafood platter and those incredible desserts. Would you believe carrot, strawberry cake, and Reese's peanut butter and Snickers pies? They even serve a sugar-free cherry pie that owner Lee Collins swears has no sugar. But it's the apple dumpling a la mode served on a hot dish, topped with ice cream and a cinnamon glaze that is the show stopper.

"When folks finish a meal with us we keep a dolly around to wheel people to their car," joked Collins.

DINERS INFORMATION

Address:
101 N. Front Street
Hours:
Open, 6:00 a.m. – 8:00 p.m., Monday –Thursday
6:00 a.m. – 10:00p.m., Friday and Saturday
8:00 a.m. – 4:00 p.m., Sunday
Phone:
606/886-1744
Price Range: $
Area Attractions:
Jenny Wiley State Park, Stone Crest Golf Course

Chirico Ristorante

Sometime the best places to eat pop up in the least expected places. It happens all over Kentucky, and one of those is located on a narrow side street in downtown Pikeville.

A word of caution: do not go here unless you're hungry. The portions served are among the largest of any restaurants in this book.

Chirico, an Italian eatery, is located in the old Pinson Hotel which still operates as a hotel. The walls are covered in a 1950s knotty pine paneling topped off with a family photo history on the wall.

"Most of our recipes are old family ones handed down for three generations," says Frank Chirico, Jr., who operates the restaurant.

The menu choices are almost too many. It begins with appetizers and unlimited hot bread sticks, plus soups and salads. The Italian wedding soup is something special. With a tomato base, assorted vegetables, pasta and Italian sausage, a cup may not be enough. Better order a bowl.

The traditional Italian dishes are the highlight, but this mega menu includes steaks, shrimp, chicken, calzones, and sandwiches. There is one dish that you've got to order, particularly if you're here strictly for the Italian. It is appropriately named "Tour of Italy." It is served on a rather large plate

filled with lasagna, spaghetti, meatballs, rigatoni, manicotti and a baby calzone. With this, of course, comes a salad and garlic breadsticks.

The regulars here are easy to spot. Couples order one main dish, split it, and a couple of salads.

Beer and wine are available.

The desserts are equally impressive. The cannoli is an Italian pastry filled with sweet cream cheese, chocolate chips and drizzled with your choice of syrup. There's also tiramisu and spumoni which is chocolate, pistachio and cherry nut Italian ice cream with a drizzle of strawberry and chocolate sauce.

DINERS INFORMATION

Address:
136 Pike Street
Hours:
Open, 10:00 a.m. – 9:00 p.m., Monday – Thursday
10:00 a.m. – 10:00 p.m., Friday
3:00 p.m. - 10:00 p.m., Saturday
Closed Sunday
Phone:
606/432-7070
Price Range: $$
Area Attractions:
Hatfield-McCoy Festival

EASTERN

Courthouse Café

Lots of restaurants are located in historic buildings, but that doesn't necessarily mean they are good. There's one, however, that is and it's in Whitesburg, Kentucky.

The Courthouse Café sits across from the Letcher County Courthouse, right smack in the middle of town in a 1911 building that originally housed a bank.

Owners Josephine Richardson and Laura Schuster, on the surface might seem unlikely restaurant proprietors in the mountains of eastern Kentucky, but when you taste the food they turn out and see the warm, upscale ambience they have created with the exposed brick walls and pressed-tin ceilings, it all makes sense.

Richardson comes from an "up-East" Italian family in Connecticut and New York City, while Schuster grew up hanging around Frankfort and Lexington in the restaurant business while attending college.

They love to cook, and the benefactors are the locals in Whitesburg and anyone who visits the Courthouse Café.

Since 1985 Schuster and Richardson have made a name for themselves in eastern Kentucky.

The restaurant is known for offering five different daily lunch specials that often includes a pasta, meat-and-two, soup and sandwich, salad, and vegetarian plate. Naturally, they offer an assortment of sandwiches on their menu that includes made-from-scratch hamburgers.

Dinner at the Courthouse Café in the words of Josephine Richardson, "slows down a bit."

"We do the very best we can to provide fresh and in season whenever possible," she says.

You can't go wrong with the New York strip or seafood that includes grilled rainbow trout, Tilapia and salmon. The chef also offers up a pork tenderloin and several different preparations of grilled chicken breasts.

Richardson is quick to point out that desserts are very important at the Courthouse Café, especially the Tanglewood Pie. It's a combination of a baked pie crust, covered with sliced bananas, topped with a cream cheese filling and whipped cream. And on top of that add a "flip" of sugar with a little vanilla and a blueberry topping.

If that's not your choice, perhaps it will be the butterscotch or chocolate fudge brownies accompanied by a scoop of ice cream.

DINERS INFORMATION

Address:
104 North Webb Avenue
Hours:
Open, 10:00 a.m. – 8:30 p.m., Monday-Friday
Phone:
606/633-5859
Price Range: $
Area Attractions:
Pine Mountain Trail, Seco Winery

EASTERN

Frances' Diner

HAZARD, KENTUCKY

Frances Napier is a busy lady. She has a hand in just about all of the main dishes served at her restaurant, which is open 24 hours a day, seven days a week. You guessed it. She works sometime 18 hours a day making sure she provides her customers with the best food possible.

"Our whole menu is made pretty much from scratch," she says. "And our full menu is available 24 hours a day except for our daily specials."

The menu presents soup beans, salmon patties, kraut wieners, fried chicken, chicken and dumplings, ocean perch, catfish, spaghetti, steak and gravy, fried green tomatoes and an assortment of desserts that make you want to take some home, even when you're full.

How about butterscotch, Kentucky silk, apple and pecan pies? How about carrot cake, raspberry nut cake, hot fudge cake, and of course, cheesecake? And they're all homemade.

Frances' Diner is a family restaurant even though it has two pool tables.

"We've had them here ever since we opened," Napier said. "The kids like to play and that's fine with us."

Frances' Diner daily specials keep the regular customers coming back again and again. The meats will change, but those delicious fresh vegetables will pretty much stay the same.

Although everyday is good, Napier adds that her customers really like Thursdays when she serves turkey and dressing. And then there's the meatloaf.

"People around here say we have the best in town," she says. "With the amount of food we serve we have to cook all day long and we serve it til we run out."

Napier has been in the restaurant business for 42 years and at her present location for 15 years, so you better believe she knows her way around the kitchen.

Address:
449 Chester St.
Hours:
Open 24 hours a day
Closed Thanksgiving and Christmas Day
Phone:
606/436-0090
Price Range: $
Area Attractions:
Buckhorn Lake

Harland Sanders Cafe

CORBIN, KENTUCKY

Harland Sanders Café is the lone exception of a chain restaurant being in the book. The KFC sign out front indicates that this is, indeed a chain. However, in another sense it's not.

This is where the Colonel originally started it all. It's a historical site and a place where you need to visit and see this museum–like building that once served as a restaurant and motel on U.S. 25 in the 1940's. In fact it was Duncan Hines who helped Col. Sanders get his start when he listed the Corbin restaurant in his 1939 travel guide as a "good place to eat."

The restaurant has been restored even to the point of exhibits depicting the original kitchen, and another showing what one of the motel rooms looked like.

The dining room is full of tributes to the Colonel as it related to his life and travels throughout the world.

Restaurant owner John R. Neal is proud of the fact that of all of the great food franchises, this is the only one that still operates as a restaurant.

"The original McDonald's and the very first Pizza Hut are no longer restaurants," Neal pointed out. "But our restaurant here is still going strong and one of the tops in the country."

This restaurant has been saved from those who want something newer and brighter in order to keep up with all of the "others". It was saved from being torn down.

Harland Sanders Café is a big bite of Americana and definitely a must see. Why wouldn't anyone want a piece of the Colonel's secret recipe in the very spot where it all began?

"Harland Sanders Café," says Neal, "stands today restored and preserved as a landmark in the history of American commerce. There is so much that is unique here, and it all points to the uniqueness of Harland Sanders."

DINERS INFORMATION

Directions:
Intersection of U.S. 25 West and 25 East
Hours:
Open, 10:00 a.m. – 10:00 p.m., daily
Phone:
606/528-2163
Price Range: $
Area Attractions:
Cumberland Falls

Kathy's Country Kitchen

CLAY CITY, KENTUCKY

It says "Fried Green Tomatoes" on the front window. "It's what we are really known for," says owner Kathy Reed. "So they better be good."

And they are! In fact they are better than good.

Kathy's is located just off of the Bert Combs Mountain Parkway in Clay City. It's a rather large restaurant, seating about 130. There's plenty of room to eat some good ole home cooking. Big round, oak tables with four high-back oak chairs, provides customers with plenty of elbow room.

The menu offers a large selection of burgers, sandwiches and soups. Steaks and seafood are very popular on the dinner menu.

At lunchtime a meat and two plus salad and corn bread is the highlight.

Breakfast also makes Kathy's a busy place. From omelets to pancakes to country ham to tenderloin to biscuits & gravy, the choices are plenty.

Here are some selections you might want to strongly consider. The Manhattan roast beef open face sandwich will not disappoint. Neither will the pot roast and dressing with a side of broccoli casserole. And the fried chicken is skillet fried and the pork chops are hand breaded.

214

As you might expect from Kathy's Country Kitchen you can order such traditional southern foods as pinto beans, fried apples, potato cakes, baked sweet potato, chicken livers, cooked cabbage, beef stew, meatloaf and pickled beets.

Desserts include pumpkin cheesecake, lemon pie, chocolate pie and yellow cake with caramel.

Address:
20 Black Creek Road
Hours:
Open, 6:00 a.m. – 10:00 p.m. daily
Phone:
606/663-4179
Price Range: $
Area Attractions:
Red River Gorge

Miss Ida's Tea Room

At one time Inez in Martin County might have been rather difficult to reach. Years ago the lack of good roads prevented this eastern Kentucky town from being what some might consider the mainstream of public access. Not any more!

A beautiful four-lane highway gently meanders through the scenic mountains from Prestonsburg on Rt. 3.

And when you arrive at Miss Ida's Team Room, they are there to greet you and meet your dining needs in a big way.

Ida Davis oversees the eatery with assistance from daughter Linda, Manager Melanie Harmon and assistant Hazel Smith.

Inez is a small town of just over 600 people, not far from the West Virginia line in what is considered "coal country," and for a small town you just don't expect to find a restaurant like Ida's. Oh sure, it has your comfort foods but on weekends the restaurant and Chef Wes shows off its fancy side.

To go along with Ida's upscale atmosphere of cloth napkins, beautiful carpet, and plush seating, Chef Wes offers a limited number of two different specials on Friday and Saturday nights.

It's almost guaranteed that you have never had such an awesome serving of Prime Rib. No pre-cooked here. It's cooked to order and there is barely room on the plate for the baked potato that comes with it. The second Friday night special is shrimp with carbonara sauce served over bow tie pasta. Both specials come with sautéed vegetables on a separate plate.

216

The soups are minestrone and a creamy chicken and rice that are so thick it could probably be served as a dip.

Did we mention the bread pudding? You won't believe it. Served hot with a whiskey-caramel sauce topping, it's a meal in itself.

Even if you can't get to Ida's Tea Room on a weekend, the rest of the week features menu items like spaghetti, chicken alfredo, roasted pork loin, rib eye steak, T-bones and fried shrimp.

An assortment of sandwiches and salads are also available.

DINERS INFORMATION

Address:
1432 Main Street
Hours:
Open, Monday – Thursday, 11:00 a.m. – 8:00 p.m.
Friday, 11:00 a.m. – 9:00 p.m.
Saturday, 4:00 p.m. – 9:00 p.m.
Closed Sunday
Phone:
606/298-3727
Price Range: $$
Area Attractions:
Yatesville Lake

Mona's Restaurant

Don't go to Mona's Restaurant looking for burgers and fries. In fact nothing at Mona's is fried.

This Pikeville eatery is not necessarily a health food restaurant, but it is a healthy restaurant. . .and it's good.

There's a large selection of cold and hot sandwiches as well as salads, soups and would you believe cholesterol free, low calorie peanut butter fudge!

And speaking of peanut butter, you'll want to try the peanut butter sandwich. It has wheat germ, banana on whole wheat bread with a little honey.

Ann Thompson who represents the family as the general manager of Mona's likes to point out that their customers can eat healthy and the food still is good.

Hot sandwiches include tuna melt, hot ham, roast beef and turkey melt. Most are served on low carb bread.

Mona's is such a welcome change of pace for those who like to eat out. The chicken salad plate, grilled chicken salad, and the sprout salad (bed of alfalfa sprouts covered with a special dressing and sprinkled with sunflower seed and topped with chunks of cheese) are just some of your choices.

The soups are chili, beef vegetable and creamy potato.

Mona's also has something for the so-called sweet tooth in the way of Adkin's Cheese Cake, and their list of special drinks include a long list of cappuccinos as well as such

things called Tropical Delight, Strawberry Supreme, and Islander.

"And if that's not enough we can add rocket fuel to any of our drinks," says Ann Thompson. "It's a few drops of liquid herbs for added energy and vitality."

Mona's is a clean, crisp restaurant with green and cream checkerboard tile flooring and seats about 45.

Of all the wonderful, healthy food items sold at Mona's, it's the fudge and pasta salad that Thompson says are the most popular.

"Our pasta has 57 herbs and spices in it and no one else has anything like it," she says.

Gourmet gift baskets are for sale. They can be made up with fudge, peanuts, jams, jellies and dressings.

DINERS INFORMATION

Address:
278 Town Mountain Road
Hours:
Open, Monday – Friday, 9:00 a.m. – 9:00 p.m.
Saturday, 10:00 a.m. – 9:00 p.m.
Closed Sunday
Phone:
606/437-MONA
Price Range: $
Area Attractions:
Hatfield-McCoy Festival

Opal's
MCKEE, KENTUCKY

Opal's is a comfort food haven. If a customer wants something prepared a certain way Kathy Carpenter and her staff will do their best to accommodate.

Breakfast is a big deal. You can order it anytime the restaurant is open. And when you visit Opal's you may want to avoid the one round table. Especially if you get there early in the morning. It's okay mind you if you want to sit next to it, however, because that's where all of the locals hang out to discuss the latest politics, rumors and gossip. So if you're sitting nearby, you could learn something.

Breakfast at Opal's runs from biscuits and gravy, to omelets to country ham to grits to French toast. If you don't see it, they'll fix it.

The sandwich menu features 31 sandwiches to choose from. They can be ordered individually or as a platter.

"We hand pat our burgers," says Carpenter. "And they are fresh."

The dinner menu is very affordable and ranges from grilled pork chops, oysters, shrimp and country ham to T-bones and Rib-eyes.

There's also a buffet and salad bar which is served everyday except Saturday.

Kathy says probably the two most popular menu items are the Philly Hoagie, a loaded sandwich with shredded steak, grilled onions, peppers and mozzarella cheese, and then there is the "Lite Side"

marinated grilled chicken served with potato, slaw and grilled garlic bread.

Opal's offers only one dessert, so it better be good. It's the homemade cream pie and it is available in chocolate, coconut, butterscotch and lemon.

"The locals buy them instead of birthday cakes," says Carpenter. "It's my mom's recipe from 21 years ago."

Her mom's name? Opal.

Address:
Highway 89 & Water Street
Hours:
Open, 6:00 a.m. – 9:00 p.m., 7 days a week
Phone:
606/287-1530
Price Range: $
Area Attractions:
Horse Lick Creek Biosphere

Teapot Cafe

HINDMAN, KENTUCKY

The Teapot Café in Hindman sits so close to the road on Hwy. 160, just outside the city limit sign, that it's a little difficult to see as you round the curve for first time. But it's worth turning around. All of the locals, however, are accustomed to seeing the large sandwich-board-type sign that barely sits off the edge of the highway. It advertises 'The Teapots' daily specials to passing motorist.

Mima Bolen knows cooking - - country cooking to be precise, and because of it, anyone who eats there gets to experience good old down home food.

"We do things different here," she says. "I cook and prepare my food to my taste, not a regular recipe."

She, daughter Erica and son Eric, even peel and mash the potatoes in order to make everything as fresh as possible. The cornbread, soups, chili, pies, cakes and fudge are all made from scratch.

"We send our fudge all over the world," Mima proudly adds. "And some of our customers actually come in twice a day to get it."

Her day usually begins at 5 a.m. every morning. She buys her vegetables fresh everyday. No buying in bulk here. "We're a small restaurant," she says.

It's those daily specials that get all of the locals excited. The phone rings constantly asking "what's being served and if there's any peanut butter pie left?"

"The jowl bacon-soup bean with fried potatoes, cornbread and onion is a sell-out," Mima offers. "They come from

all over. And when I do turkey and dressing I stay here all night in order to keep an eye on everything."

Just for the record, the Teapot's pan fried chicken with corn meal gravy ranks right up there with any you've ever tasted.

Now if all of this incredibly good food doesn't strike your fancy, there's always the chili dog. Wow!

Mima and her family are proud of the Teapot, it shows when you walk in the door where you see an old cook stove and little teapots everywhere.

"We even made the dining guide in the Lexington Herald," she says proudly.

Address:
1797 Hwy. 160
Hours:
Monday – Friday, 11:00 a.m. – 8:00 p.m.
Closed Saturday
Sunday, 11:00 a.m. – 3:00 p.m.
Phone:
606/785-9899
Price Range: $
Area Attractions:
Appalachian Artisan Center

Weavers Hot Dogs

When you go to Weavers don't expect anything fancy. It's not. But when you go you can expect one of the best chili dogs you've eaten this side of the Rockies.

Owner Carl David Weaver is a third generation Weaver's Hot Dog at the local landmark that sits smack in the middle of downtown on Main Street. There's no special parking or drive-thru so you've got to hunt for a parking space.

At Weaver's "it's all about the chili," and Carl and his mom and dad are the only ones who know the 65-year-old recipe that Carl, his grandfather, came up with in 1941.

You can get a hamburger at Weaver's, and you can also get a grilled chicken and grilled cheese. They're good. But it's the chili dogs that are in demand, and when you step up to the service counter to place your order, when you say hot dog, it automatically comes with the chili. At Weaver's there's no such thing as a plain hot dog, so don't even order one.

Weaver says it's not unusual to go through 30 dozen dogs a day. To save you the time of multiplying that's 360 hot dogs a day.

Carl's dad, Drew, ran the restaurant from 1951 until just a few years ago, and for the most part there has been little change in the décor or the food. That's the way their customers like it.

"The old-timers will come in and tell me the food still taste the same as when my grandfather ran it," Carl says with a smile on his face. "They like it that way and so do I."

Almost just as much a part of Weaver's as the hot dogs are the several hundred pictures on the wall. It's like a history of London and Laurel

224

County. There's Carl's grandfather, dad, policemen, firemen, doctors, lawyers, soldiers, some date back to the 1920's.

At Weaver's the food doesn't hit the grill until it's ordered. The only thing prepared in advance is that famous chili.

Carl likes to tell the story of how travelers passing through London on Hwy. 25 before the days of the interstate would jump out of their cars run in Weaver's and order several hot dogs and then run and catch up to their car. That's how backed up the traffic was then.

Lots of famous Kentuckians have dined on the rock-hard wooden-seated booths over the years, and eaten off of the small paper plates, and drank from the styrofoam cups. Among them have been several governors, former UK basketball coach Joe B. Hall, and former broadcaster Cawood Ledford. They were there for the hot dogs and that chili.

DINERS INFORMATION

Address:
Main Street
Hours:
Open, 8:00 a.m. — 3:00 p.m., Monday — Friday
10:00 a.m. — 3:00 p.m., Saturday
Phone:
606/864-9937
Price Range: $
Area Attractions:
Levi Jackson State Park

Wilma's

PAINTSVILLE, KENTUCKY

Wilma Eldridge has been in the restaurant business at 212 Court Street in downtown Paintsville since 1964, so she must be doing something right. The right thing is that her restaurant is a family tradition, beginning with her mother, known as "Granny". It was Granny who helped with the recipes for those delicious coconut cream pies, butterscotch pies, and custard, pecan, apple and cherry pies. She taught her family well, because Wilma has involved two of her daughters, daughter-in-laws and now the grandchildren.

"Our customers like the personal attention they get here," Wilma says. "When most of the locals walk through the door I already know what they want."

The Johnson County restaurant has a daily buffet that offers a choice of meats and an assortment of vegetables. And those pies, delish! They are baked fresh daily and don't stay around long. When you go to Wilma's you may want to order your pie when you order the rest of your meal. If you don't, you may not get any.

Fried chicken, bar-b-que ribs, liver and onions, meatloaf and roast beef are staple items that are alternated on the buffet.

Wilma points out there are a couple of things on the menu that are real special. She begins with the roast beef special, served Manhattan style with sliced bread topped with mashed potatoes and gravy. An order of slaw

comes with it. "We've had this same item on our menu since we opened our doors over 42 years ago," she says.

She also talks about the Yankee Special, a triple decker club sandwich, created several years ago when the New York Yankee baseball team had a minor league club in Paintsville. It's loaded with ham, turkey, bacon, and cheese and dressed with lettuce, tomato and mayo.

Wilma's does breakfast all day, lunch and early dinner. If breakfast is your pleasure be sure and ask for some strawberry preserves. You won't regret it.

They're open seven days a week.

DINERS INFORMATION

Address:
212 Court Street
Hours:
Monday through Friday, 7:00 a.m. – 7 :00p.m.
Saturday and Sunday, 7:00a.m. – 4:00 p.m.
Phone:
606/789-5911
Price Range: $
Area Attractions:
Paintsville Lake, Loretta Lynn's Home

About the Author

Gary P. West grew up in Elizabethtown, Kentucky and attended Western Kentucky University before graduating from the University of Kentucky with a degree in journalism in 1967.

At UK he was a daily sports editor for the *Kentucky Kernel*.

Later he served as editor for the nation's largest civilian enterprise military newspaper at Fort Bragg, North Carolina. From there he went to work as an advertising copywriter in the corporate office of one the country's largest insurance companies, State Farm Insurance in Bloomington, Illinois.

In 1972 he returned to Kentucky where he began publishing an advertising shopper in Bowling Green.

Along the way, for twelve years, he worked in the athletic department as executive director of the Hilltopper Athletic Foundation at Western Kentucky University, and provided color commentary on the Hilltopper Basketball Network.

In 1993 he became executive director of the Bowling Green Area Convention and Visitors Bureau, where he solidified his background in hospitality. He is a freelance writer for several magazines in addition to writing a syndicated newspaper column, *Out & About... Kentucky Style*, for a number of papers across the state.

In 2005 he wrote the highly acclaimed book, *King Kelly Coleman–Kentucky's Greatest Basketball Legend*.

Index